T0064877

MY KINGDOM FOR A HORSE

MY KINGDOM FOR A HORSE

THE WAR OF THE ROSES

ED WEST

Skyhorse Publishing

Skyhorse Publishing books may be purchased in bulk at special discounts for sales promotion, corporate gifts, fund-raising, or educational purposes. Special editions can also be created to specifications. For details, contact the Special Sales Department, Skyhorse Publishing, 307 West 36th Street, 11th Floor, New York, NY 10018 or info@skyhorsepublishing.com.

Skyhorse® and Skyhorse Publishing® are registered trademarks of Skyhorse Publishing, Inc.®, a Delaware corporation.

Visit our website at www.skyhorsepublishing.com.

10 9 8 7 6 5 4 3 2 1

Library of Congress Cataloging-in-Publication Data is available on file.

Cover design by Rain Saukas

Print ISBN: 978-1-5107-1989-7
Ebook ISBN: 978-1-5107-1994-1

Printed in the United States of America

Contents

Introduction

*N*ow is the winter of our discontent/Made glorious summer by this sun of York. As the historian Robert Tombs put it, no other country but England had, until the age of cinema, turned its national history into a popular drama, thanks to William Shakespeare's series of plays. These eight histories chart the country's dynastic conflict from 1399 to 1485, starting with the overthrow of the demented Richard II and climaxing with death of the hunchbacked villain Richard III at the Battle of Bosworth.

Richard II, known to history as being deliriously paranoid—although, as it turned out, they *were* out to get him—was replaced by his cousin, the Duke of Lancaster, who took the throne as Henry IV. Then, over a period of thirty years starting in 1455, three more kings died violently, seven royal princes were killed in battle, and five more executed or murdered; thirty-one peers or their heirs also fell in the field, and twenty others were put to death. It ended when Henry Tudor, distantly related and with an extremely dubious claim, was able to take the throne as Henry VII, largely on account of still breathing. Shakespeare wrote his plays, called the Henriad, under Tudor's granddaughter Elizabeth, partly as a form of propaganda.

In the bard's telling, the overthrow of Richard II begins this chain of events, the Bishop of Carlisle warning that if the king is removed 'the blood of English shall manure the ground.' However, the conflict that later became known as the War of the Roses only began in the 1450s, following English defeat in France, which led to an enormous number of extremely violent men returning home with widespread anger at the way the country was being mismanaged.

The cause of this was the insanity of Henry VI, and his weak, financially incompetent rule. In the absence of a strong king, power rested with 'affinities' of related aristocrats and their soldiers, a Mafia society in which the ordinary people had little legal protection. The richest aristocrats commanded vast armies and led them into battle under their banners—the White Lion of Mortimer, the Bear of the Earl of Warwick, the White Swan of the Duke of Buckingham, the Falcon and Fetterlock for Richard of York, or the Sun in Splendor for his son Edward. Where their men would go drinking, the landlords began to display their symbols by the entrance, which is how English ale houses and taverns—and so many of today's pubs—got their names.[1]

The title of the conflict gives it a romantic feel that probably wasn't as apparent to those on the battlefield having swords shoved into their eyes. Henry IV's great-grandfather Edmund Crouchback, the brother of King Edward I, had been a crusader, and like many fighting the holy war, took the red rose as his emblem; much later Edward III's son Edmund, the first Duke of York, adopted the white rose as his. For this reason, the dynastic struggle in the following century is known as the War of the Roses, although neither side wore the emblems in battle, and the term wasn't used at the time. By Shakespeare's period, it was known as the Quarrel of the Warring Roses and the War between the Two Roses, although the exact phrase 'the War or the Roses' is attributed to historical novelist Sir Walter Scott in 1829.[2] However, the idea of the flowers representing the warring families went back to the fifteenth century, if not the exact wording.[3] After Bosworth, Henry VII married the Yorkist Edward IV's daughter Elizabeth and symbolized the end of the conflict by having a new emblem created that intertwined the red rose of the House of Lancaster with the white rose of the House of York.[4]

By that stage, there was barely anyone left to fight; between 1455 and 1471, twenty-six peers were killed in battle, and thirteen were executed, while six of Edward III's descendants in the male line had died violently in the conflict.[5] Out of seventy adult peers in the period, fifty are known to have fought in battles 'they had to win if they wanted to survive.'[6] Contemporary Philippe de Commynes wrote that 'there have been seven or eight memorable battles in England, and sixty or eighty princes and lords of the blood have died violently.' In 1460–61 alone, twelve noblemen were killed in the field and six were beheaded, a third of the English higher peerage; three dukes of Somerset died violently in a short space of time, while four generations of Percy heirs fell in battle, and four Percy brothers died violently within four short years; four members of the Courtenay family in the direct line also died between 1461 and 1471. Although by one calculation there were only twelve or thirteen weeks spent fighting spanning thirty-two years, it was enough to kill off many noble families.

It also saw the complete abandonment of chivalry, the old law regarding warfare which stated that although you could basically kill the common soldiers as much as you liked, horsemen—*chevalier*—were supposed to spare aristocratic prisoners. This code had begun to break down in the fourteenth century and, by the time of the War of the Roses, the likes of Edward IV would order their troops to 'spare the commons, kill the gentles,' a reverse of traditional rules. After the battles, countless noblemen and knights were executed, part of a cycle of revenge in which the common soldiers didn't feature as targets.

The fourteenth century Flemish chronicler Froissart wrote of the English: 'They take delight in battles and slaughters.' And for aristocrats, that might have been true, but for most of the population, who weren't caught up in the feuds, life went on pretty much as normal. There was no ideological or religious meaning to the war, and civilians were never targeted; in fact, life was pretty good for most. Military leaders made sure armies did not damage the countryside, since there was nothing to be gained from it, and private house building continued as before. Direct taxation, which normally shoots up during war, actually decreased during this conflict.[7] In fact, a better analogy than the Mafia might be soccer hooliganism—an entirely consensual activity in which groups of violent men beat each other up just for the fun of it.

The conflict is sometimes very hard to follow, largely because almost every man involved is called either Henry, Richard, or Edward, which makes it as terrible as a soap opera. Secondly, most of the combatants are also referred to by their titles, such as York or Warwick, some changed titles during the course of the conflict, and to make things even *more* confusing, sometimes the battles would take place near the town after which a one of the players is named (York was killed near York alongside Salisbury and Rutland, while his son was in Salisbury). Warwick's actual name was Richard Neville, also the name of his father, the Earl of Salisbury, who was also killed near York, alongside York.

There were also three different earls of Warwick during the period, all completely different in character, and several Somersets. Also, to make it more confusing, the families involved had such a heavy death toll that one aristocrat would be killed and then his son or brother—often with the same title—would die in a battle a couple of years later, leaving the reader to wonder if he hadn't just been killed on the previous page. And thirdly, since this was a war among the inbred descendants of Edward III's five sons, all the participants were related to one another at least twice over, making the family tree utterly baffling. For that reason I tend to refer to people by their best-known titles, unless to distinguish between two brothers.

It all begins in 1399 with a dispute between two cousins, grandsons of King Edward, called Richard and Henry.

CHAPTER ONE

Heavy is the Head that Wears the Crown

The story begins with Edward III, probably the greatest warrior in English history, who was hugely popular for leading the country into an almost never-ending war with France in 1337; later called the Hundred Years' War, although it was even longer than that.

Centuries earlier, Edward's ancestor Henry II had, through inheritance and marriage, ruled over a huge but incoherent group of territories including England and the French regions of Normandy, Anjou, and Aquitaine, an entity since called the Angevin Empire. Unfortunately, his hopeless and drunken coward of a son King John, famous in English history for issuing Magna Carta, had lost almost all of his continental possessions in 1204, leaving only Gascony, the southern portion of Aquitaine. However, the French claimed even this, and when France's King Philippe VI invaded Gascony in 1337 Edward could not make war on him because, as Duke of Aquitaine, he was a vassal of the French monarch. To declare war against an overlord would risk excommunication by the pope, and so Edward instead claimed the throne of France, through his mother Isabella, the daughter of a previous monarch, Philippe IV. By today's rules of succession, Edward had a better claim, but at that time inheritance was not so simple, and the French reasoned that the throne could not pass through the female line.

The war saw some stunning English victories, at Crecy (1346) and Poitiers (1356), won respectively by King Edward and his eldest son Edward, the Black Prince. Although France was far larger and in most ways more advanced, the English had longbows, a new weapon that had originated in Wales and which could fire up to twelve arrows a minute at great speed and force. Before Poitiers, the medieval order was built on cavalry, which ensured aristocratic power, since being a knight was expensive; however, anyone could fire a bow and arrow, so long as they were prepared to give themselves spinal injuries through years of practice (which the English king made compulsory).

For three decades France was devastated by marauding armies, but for the English, Edward III seemed the greatest king of all time. He was unconditionally supported by the Lords and Commons despite the huge cost in both lives and money for the war. With five surviving sons and three daughters, most of them married to heirs and heiresses from among the sixty families that comprised the English aristocracy, he seemed to have laid the foundations of a great dynasty. However, a peace treaty in 1360 failed and the war dragged on, with ever more pointless raids by the English getting nowhere; the Black Prince fell ill and Edward III had a series of strokes, dying in 1377 a gibbering imbecile, a year after his eldest son.

To top off a fantastic century for France, while all of this was going on, Europe was hit by the Black Death, a ghastly, agonizing disease that killed between one-third and one-half of the continent's population after days of lingering agony; this was after one in ten people had starved to death in the Great Famine of 1315.

Edward's successor, the Black Prince's son Richard II, had what we'd today call a few personal 'issues.' When he was born in Bordeaux, he just happened to be attended by three kings, of Castile,

Portugal, and Navarre, and this seems to have given him a few ideas. He commissioned paintings of himself standing next to John the Baptist and St. Edward the Confessor, and claimed to have discovered a vial of oil given by the Virgin Mary to St. Thomas Becket, the archbishop of Canterbury whose head was smashed in by Henry II's men.

Richard favored peace with France, because war was expensive and compromised his power by forcing him to ask Parliament for money. He believed in a new idea coming from Italy: the divine rights of kings, which suggested that monarchs were no longer just the strongest warlords, but also chosen by God Himself. His opponents weren't so keen on the idea, especially not if God had chosen Richard. The king insisted on being addressed not as 'my lord,' as was traditional, but with more extravagant titles such as 'your most puissant prince,' and would sit for hours in silence with courtiers who were forbidden to make eye contact with him.

His most powerful subject was Edward III's middle son John of Gaunt, but after Richard's uncle went off to Spain to try to become king there, a dangerous rift opened between Richard and his opponents, led by his youngest uncle Thomas of Woodstock. Woodstock and four other powerful lords became known as the Lords Appellant, because they were appealing against the king.

It came to a head in 1387 when Richard's crony Robert de Vere, the Earl of Oxford, was defeated in battle by the five Appellants, and the following year their 'Merciless Parliament' vindictively had a number of the king's followers and friends put to death or exiled. Richard was still barely out of his teens and was scarred by these events; he would later become totally deranged.

However, some relatively good years followed, and the chronicler Thomas Walsingham was able to write in 1397: 'That year, the kingdom seemed to be on the verge of enjoying a period of great stability, partly because of the Royal marriages and the riches accumulated in aid of that, but also on account of the long truce with

France, and the presence of so many noblemen, more numerous and higher in rank than any other realm could produce.' One of those predictions political pundits are subsequently embarrassed by.

That year Richard's three main enemies, Thomas of Woodstock, Warwick, and Arundel, were summoned to a banquet, but only Warwick accepted: he was immediately arrested. Richard, upon taking full control as an adult in 1388, had proclaimed that he had put all bitterness behind him, but in fact the king had waited a full nine years before getting his revenge. His uncle Thomas was strangled, Arundel was beheaded, and Warwick, after pleading for his life, according to Adam of Usk 'wailing and weeping and whining, traitor that he was,' was banished to the grim outpost of the Isle of Man where he was harshly treated by its governor, William le Scrope.

However, Richard then made a mistake in exiling his cousin Henry of Derby, called Bolingbroke by Shakespeare. Henry, along with the Earl of Mowbray, was one of the two more moderate Appellants and so had escaped punishment; however, Mowbray, the son-in-law of Arundel, apparently warned Derby they were 'on the point of being undone' by the king; he told his father, who informed Richard.

The two men accused each other of lying, and to resolve it, Richard ordered them to fight a duel. However, at the last minute he called it off and exiled Mowbray for ten years and Derby for five, promising to allow his cousin to return when his father John of Gaunt died. Both men had trained quite extensively for the event and, for his combat, Derby had special armor made in Milan, but Richard's logic was that as people regarded victory in battle as divine favor, whoever was able to knock the other off was by definition telling the truth—and if this was Mowbray it would suggest Richard *was* plotting against them. However, if Henry of Derby won then he would be innocent of treason and would be more popular than ever.

In 1399, Mowbray died in exile, as did Derby's father. William Shakespeare has Gaunt in his last days making a moving and patriotic speech to his nephew in which he speaks of:

> This royal throne of kings, this scepter'd isle,
> This earth of majesty, this seat of Mars,
> This other Eden, demi-paradise,
> This fortress built by Nature for herself,
> Against infection and the hand of war,
> This happy breed of men, this little world,
> This precious stone set in the silver sea,[8]

The above is one of the best passages in the English language, although near contemporary Thomas Gascoigne has a slightly less romantic account of the meeting between uncle and nephew, writing that one of Gaunt's last acts was to expose his 'pox-ridden genitals' to the king. He claims Gaunt 'died of a putrefaction of his genitals and body, caused by the frequenting of women, for he was a great fornicator.' Gascoigne was a theologian and might not have approved of Gaunt's famous penchant for the ladies.

When his uncle died, the king went back on his word and had Derby's lands confiscated and so, in 1399, while Richard was in Ireland trying to resolve one of the country's numerous aristocratic feuds, Derby landed in Yorkshire. He claimed he only returned to win back his personal lands, but at some point he decided he may as well become king instead; soon everyone had deserted Richard, including his dog, who licked Henry in the face when the two men met, and the king's attempt to raise a loyal army amounted to just one hundred men.

According to the kangaroo court established by the new king, Richard was overthrown on account of thirty-nine crimes, among them his 'perjuries, sodomitical acts, dispossession of his subjects, reduction of his people to servitude, lack of reason, and incapacity to rule.' He was locked up and, after an inept attempt to free him by his last remaining followers, was probably murdered. Although Richard was childless—his wife was only ten years old, in fact— by the generally accepted laws of succession Derby was not next in line to the throne, since Edward III's second son Lionel had living descendants through his only daughter Philippa. She had married a Mortimer, a powerful Welsh border family whose men were unfortunately always getting killed in fights; four generations had died young, the latest being in 1397 when Roger Mortimer was stabbed to death in Ireland, and Roger's heir Edmund was only eight.

Richard's downfall would become the start of the great Shakespearean tragedy, and it immediately became the subject of a propaganda war, which the bard was to continue. After Henry became king, he sent letters to all the abbeys and major churches 'instructing the heads of these religious houses to make available for examination all of their chronicles which touched upon the state and governance of the kingdom of England from the time of William the Conqueror up until the present day.' He obviously destroyed many records, and the chronicles of the city of London were cut with a knife, with two and a half folios from the period taken out. As a result, history has probably been too kind to Henry.

Derby, unlike his slightly odd and pale cousin, had been a heroic figure who loved traditional regal activities like jousting and crusading, and had spent time with the Teutonic Knights, a Catholic military order, fighting against pagans in northeast Europe. But almost as soon as Henry became king he turned into a tragic figure cursed with ill health and bad luck, and begun to think God had it in for him. At his coronation, as he was about to be crowned, it was discovered that his hair was covered in lice, and the special investiture ring slipped from his finger and fell down a crack, never to be seen again. The following year the plague returned, the first time since 1369.

King Henry seemed to be permanently troubled by rebellion from supporters of the deposed king, who could be identified by the white hart (a sort of deer) they wore on their coats. After one attempt to assassinate Henry and his sons, three rebel lords were lynched and twenty-six executed; another plot, in September 1401, involved placing a medieval weapon called a caltrap, with three poisoned spikes, in his bed.

These uprisings were kept going by increasingly implausible rumors that the old king was still alive, often encouraged by Henry's enemies. The king of Scotland awarded a pension to a man called 'Mummet' who claimed to be Richard but clearly wasn't; he had been found on the Hebridean Isle of Islay in 1402 and was recognized by a local woman who claimed to have seen Richard in Ireland. All in all, a rather unconvincing story, and Mummet was later revealed to be a Cambridgeshire man called Thomas Warde, one of numerous wandering charlatans who occasionally turn up in medieval history.

The depressed Scottish monarch Robert III, who described himself as 'the worst of kings and most wretched of men in the kingdom,' had good reason to oppose Henry, since the English king had declared war on Scotland almost immediately upon taking the throne because they refused to recognize him. Scotland was in chaos at the time, a 'den of thieves,' according to Walter Bower's *Scotichronicon*; Robert's brother the Duke of Albany had seized power while another brother, Alexander, had gone on a rampage by burning down Elgin Cathedral, becoming known as the Wolf of Badenoch. Then the English invaded, Henry becoming the last English king to do so. Nothing was achieved and while in Scotland, Henry heard about an uprising in Wales.

In 1400, a nobleman called Owain Glyndwr had proclaimed himself Prince of Wales. Glyndwr was portrayed by Shakespeare as a wild man living in a world of magic and pixies, as that was how people viewed the Welsh at the time, but in real life he came from mixed English-Welsh gentry from the border and was a true European prince, as well as a skilled diplomat. He spoke French, Latin, and English and had studied law at the Inns of Court in London under the patronage of the Earl of Arundel, and had fought on campaign for Richard II in Scotland.

But he was also heir to the princes of Powys, his father Gruffydd Fychan II having been 'hereditary Tywysog of Powys Fadog,' (a sort of prince) and kept their traditions, employing bards and harpists, and believing in ancient Welsh prophecies about the expulsion of the Saxons from Britain (the Welsh always believed each uprising would be the one that finally defeated the English after one thousand years, despite all evidence to the contrary).

Owain was persuasive and charming, and he won over not only the French and leading churchmen, but several English barons who became sympathetic to his cause. Glyndwr defeated an English army in 1401, which they blamed on 'the evil arts of Franciscan friars' who had 'forged links with demons.' Again in 1402, Glyndwr won a victory against the English, at Bryn Glas in Powys, and captured Edmund Mortimer, a great-grandson of Edward III and one of the leading landholders in the border area. Mortimer's own Welsh troops had changed sides and so the English prisoner was led into Wales.

Despite Mortimer being the king's cousin, Henry refused to pay the ransom, so instead he married the Welsh leader's daughter and joined him. Henry's miserliness also helped alienate Mortimer's in-laws, the Percys, who happened to be the most powerful family in the North.

The Percys had arrived in England alongside William the Conqueror in 1066 and, as earls of Northumberland, they controlled the border with Scotland. The Percy family had supported Derby when he'd arrived in 1399, and they may have felt a bit misled, although they had been rewarded. The king had appointed Henry Percy, the Earl of Northumberland, as Constable of England and Lord of

Man, while the earl's eldest son—also Henry—became justiciar of north Wales, responsible for enforcing English law in that region. Meanwhile, Northumberland's brother Thomas, Earl of Worcester, was made steward of the royal household. But they were discontent nonetheless. The earl's son, who was known as Harry Hotspur by the Scots because of the speed in which he rode into battle, was a particularly belligerent individual who had first experienced battle at the age of nine, something not considered especially odd (although child psychologists today don't normally recommend it).

In September 1402, a Scottish force led by Archibald, Earl of Douglas had rolled over the border, only to be defeated by the Percys at Homildon Hill. The king demanded that their prisoners, including Douglas, be sent to London for ransom, which the Percys took as an insult, further aggravated when he refused to ransom Mortimer.

Hotspur was persuaded to join the Welsh and marched south, the plan being to capture the king's heir Prince Henry in Shrewsbury and then join Glyndwr and proclaim Mortimer's thirteen-year-old nephew, confusingly also called Edmund Mortimer, as king. (This younger Mortimer was the Earl of March, and heir presumptive to Richard II.) To make matters more confusing, Earl Douglas had also now joined the Percys, after all the trouble he had caused in the first place.

The king reacted quickly and reached the border town of Shrewsbury with fourteen thousand troops. Because he fully expected to be a target, the monarch had two rather unfortunate men dressed in royal surcoats as look-alikes, and predictably both of them were killed in the ensuing battle. The Earl of Douglas is supposed to have exclaimed 'Have I not slain two king Henries [*sic*] with my own hand?' At one point, the sixteen-year-old prince of Wales was hit in the face with an arrow, but survived. Hotspur was less lucky and after he was struck by an unknown archer, the king shouted 'Henry Percy is dead' and the rebels ran off.

After the battle Thomas Percy was captured, hanged, and quartered, while Hotspur's corpse was dug up, salted, and put on show in the Shrewsbury pillory, after which his head and intestines were displayed in the North. The day cost five thousand lives, and like much of this story ended up immortalized in Shakespeare's plays, although Prince Henry didn't kill Hotspur, and the two men were not the same age as the play suggests, Percy being thirty-nine.

Although Harry Hotspur was defeated, his name lives on, and not just in theater. The Percy family owned land in north London and so, in 1882, when a group of grammar schools boys wanted a name for their new soccer club, they named it after the local pub and called it Hotspur Football Club, which two years later became Tottenham Hotspur, today one of the biggest names in English sports.[9]

King Henry responded by invading Wales and passing Acts of Parliament that barred the Welsh from senior positions and confiscated lands; in the border towns of Chester and Hereford, the Prince of Wales issued city ordinances in 1403 stating that it was legal to kill any Welshman after dark with a bow and arrow. This law has never actually been repealed, but would-be assassins should note that the more relevant law against murder would still apply were anyone to try it. A similar law was passed regarding Scotsmen in York, except you couldn't shoot them on a Sunday.[10]

The spring of 1404 brought the sixth attempt to topple Henry since he seized the throne, this time led by the Countess of Oxford, mother of Richard II's former crony Robert de Vere, who was somehow convinced that Richard was alive, despite all evidence to the contrary, and wrote to the Duke of Orléans in France asking him to meet with Glyndwr at Northampton. Nothing came of it. Four years later there was yet another, more serious uprising, when the Earl of Northumberland raised an army in the North under the banner of Richard II, aided by Lord Bardolf, a baron from Norfolk; however, they were soon defeated. Northumberland was killed and Bardolf died of his wounds, and his head was stuck on a pike on London

Bridge. Glyndwr was beaten in 1410, and the following year the king was finally spared interference from France when the country's court descended into civil war.

Although inevitably doomed to defeat, Glyndwr remained a romantic figure, and in 1415 he did what all great rebels do—simply disappearing—evoking the end of King Arthur, and ensuring that the romance and legend of the last Welsh Prince of Wales would live on. A Welsh chronicle says, 'Very many say that he died; the seers maintain that he did not.' But the seers were probably wrong.

On top of these various wars, the king, who was short and angry to the point of appearing to be always on the verge of a seizure, also had disputes with Parliament, and especially its lawyers. Henry hated lawyers so much that the October 1404 assembly at Coventry was known as the 'Unlearned Parliament' or 'Parliament of Dunces,' because the king ruled that no legal experts could be elected to the Commons, because they were 'troublesome.'

There was a huge increase in the number of lawyers at the time, part of a wider economic boom that saw the city of London emerge as an important European financial center, with an increasingly wealthy commercial elite. Henry IV was the first king to invite merchants, as well as barons and bishops, to sit on the royal council, one of them being Sir Richard Whittington. Whittington was the three time mayor of London, and built the first large public toilet (for men and women together, no privacy). He also campaigned against the scandal of watered-down beer, always a vote-winner in England. However, he is probably among the best-known figures in English history simply because he became the subject of a play in the early seventeenth century and then morphed into the star of a popular pantomime. 'Panto,' as non-UK readers may not be aware, is a strange British custom where every December minor celebrities appear on stage in comical roles in plays performed with a knowing wink to the audience and references to current popular culture. They are mainly for children, but also contain lots of weird and inappropriately sexual humor for the parents forced to attend. You probably have to be British to understand.

In the panto, which traditionally centers around jokes about his name being 'Dick,' Whittington is portrayed as a poor man who is about to give up on London, but is persuaded to return by the sound of the city's Bow bells.[11] The real Dick Whittington did not come from poverty, but was a well-born exporter of woolen cloth, as well as royal dressmaker. In one year, he sold thousands of pounds worth of goods to the crown, and also made a fortune as moneylender to the king, although he once lost the royal jewels he'd taken as security, and had to forfeit the huge loan.[12]

Henry IV was so troubled by money worries that he encouraged alchemy, the art of turning base metal into gold, as a way of paying off the national debts; amazingly, it didn't work.[13] Adam of Usk wrote in 1404: 'When the Duke of Lancaster seized the crown he can have had little notion of the financial burden which was to weigh upon him for the rest of his life.' Who would have thought being king of England was such a difficult job?

He also appeared to be cursed. In May 1405, there had been further signs of discontent when Archbishop Scrope of York gathered eight thousand armed men in the city to protest taxes and the treatment of clergy, and to support his cousin Northumberland. Scrope had papers pinned to the doors of each church in York denouncing Henry as 'usurper, wastrel, and a breaker of promises,' which didn't go down well.

The king ordered Ralph Neville, the Earl of Westmorland and a rival of the Percys, to intercept the rebels; he persuaded Scrope and his allies to disband their army and said their grievances would be addressed. Then he arrested them, and Henry arrived in York and had the men immediately tried and condemned to death, with the archbishop made to ride a mule backwards on his way to his execution. Soon there were reported miracles on the spot where Scrope had been killed, and also at his tomb, while it was also said that five strips of plow land lying in ruin on the day of his execution were now producing huge quantities of grain.

And on the very evening Scrope was executed, Henry was struck down by a sudden illness near Ripon and afflicted with 'horrible torments'; he screamed that traitors were throwing fire at him, and his hands and face were covered with large red pustules. Henry's illness may have been leprosy, caught on a pilgrimage to Jerusalem, although alternative explanations are gangrene or syphilis, and although historical diagnosis is a lively field, we can never be certain. By May 1406, Henry was so sick he asked for a permanent council of seventeen men to help him run the country.

Adam of Usk described his disease as 'a rotting of the flesh, a drying up of the eyes, and a rupture of the intestines'; he had 'tumors, rashes, and suppurating flesh.' He grew heavily disfigured and would cry that he was on fire; there were swellings and rashes on his skin, and rumors abounded in France that his fingers and toes had fallen off, while the Scots got it into their heads for some reason that he had shrunk to the size of a child.

Then in 1408, on the third anniversary of the killing of Scrope, the king suffered a stroke, after which he found speech difficult; the king ordered that it be a crime to spread rumors of his poor state, which most people attributed not to a brain condition but to divine retribution for the regicide of Richard, a view shared by Henry himself. Many people also believed his second wife, Joan of Navarre, to be a practitioner of witchcraft. The king now became a chronic invalid, and Adam of Usk says he was tormented by 'festering of the flesh, dehydration of the eyes, and rupturing of internal organs.' Sometimes he couldn't speak, and at times the king thought himself dead and what he was experiencing must be hell.

Henry felt haunted by the killing of his cousin, and famously said: 'Uneasy lies the head that wears a crown' (well, Shakespeare has him saying it). At one point, everyone thought that Henry had died, and the king awoke to find his son Henry already wearing his crown, which must have made him feel appreciated. 'What right have you to this crown when I have none?' he asked him.

It had been foretold that Henry would die in Jerusalem, so he thought that as long as he avoided the place and didn't go on crusade he would be safe. While visiting the shrine of St. Edward in Westminster Abbey in 1413, he had a seizure and was carried to the Abbot's chamber, where he regained consciousness and was told he was in the Jerusalem room. 'Now I know that I shall die here in this chamber,' he replied, and did.

Haunted by the killing of his cousin, the king's last words were, 'God alone knows why I wear this crown.'

CHAPTER TWO

We Few, We Happy Few

Henry IV left four sons, the eldest of whom became Henry V, a grim-faced religious fanatic who was rather less fun than Shakespeare depicted him. Twentieth-century academic K.B. McFarlane described Henry as 'the greatest man who ever ruled England,' and despite a short reign mostly spent outside of England, he went down in history as one of the country's supreme heroes, largely thanks to the play. In reality, almost nothing about Shakespeare's depiction matches the reality of a grim-faced religious fanatic who killed thousands of innocent people in an insane, unjustified war of aggression. Henry's only recorded joke, 'War without fire is like sausages without mustard,' reflects the humor of a man who was said to almost never smile.

As with Henry of Monmouth, the prince had fallen out with his father in 1412 over the subject of war in France, which the excitable young prince was keen on. He turned up at court with an armed retinue, denouncing 'certain children of iniquity, agents of dissension, fomenters of dissension, architects of disagreement, sowers of anger and instigators of strife' who 'with serpentine cunning are hoping to alter the succession . . . and suggest we are bloodthirstily longing for the crown of England and planning a violent, abominable crime by rising up against our father.' King and prince were eventually reconciled, but the two had never got on; young Henry had actually been in Ireland with Richard II when his father invaded, and he looked up to Richard; one of his first acts as king was to order his reburial.

Henry V was raised in warfare, having been given command in Wales as a teenager, and at Shrewsbury had been scarred by a crossbow bolt that hit him just below his eye, narrowly missing his brain and spinal column. Special tongs had to be inserted to remove the arrow and it took three weeks for the wounds to heal up.[14] Being long before the age of anesthetic, this would obviously have been agonizing.

Henry was a very serious man who promoted sacred music and was interested in theology and ecclesiastical affairs. Unusual for kings in the period, he had no mistresses; in fact, from the time he ascended the throne in 1413 until his marriage eight years later, he had no sexual relations whatsoever. Even for the standards of the time he was zealously religious. In 1401 under his father, the death penalty for relapsed heretics had been brought in to target the Lollards, a rather depressing sect who followed the gloomy teachings of an Oxford cleric called John Wycliffe and denied many aspects of mainstream Catholicism, including transubstantiation (the belief that Holy Communion literally becomes the body of Christ). These proto-Protestants had once received sympathy and protection from leading aristocrats, most of all from Henry's grandfather John of Gaunt, largely because he liked their idea of appropriating Church lands and allowing aristocrats like him to take them. The killjoy aspect to Lollardy, the opposition to pilgrimages for the 'veneration of relics and images with greed and noisy excess,' was by-the-by, but when Wycliffe began to radically criticize Church doctrine, his aristocratic sympathizers dropped him like a hot stone.

Henry V had no time for such deviance. On assuming power, he had his old friend Sir John Oldcastle sentenced to death for Lollardy, although he disappeared, and later gained immortality

by becoming the model of Shakespeare's cowardly drunk Falstaff.
On one occasion, Henry personally helped burn to death a Lollard
blacksmith in a barrel; when the poor man began to scream, Henry
pulled him out and offered him a pension if he recanted, but he
refused and so went back. Henry also accused his stepmother Joan
of being a witch, and used it as an excuse to grab her land.

In fairness, he was of his time. The Catholic Church's Council of
Constance in 1414 had increased persecution of heretics, with burn-
ings and trials, while witch hunting also became popular, especially
after the 1487 treaties *Malleus Maleficarum*, which recommended the
death penalty for witchcraft, and would reach a peak with the hys-
teria of the sixteenth and early seventeenth centuries. The Church
had been going through a difficult time, as well. In the 1370s, it had
endured a schism after cardinals in Rome, under pressure from a
mob, had chosen a priest with almost no experience to be pope, who
turned out to be insane. A rival pope was picked in Avignon, a man
known as the Butcher of Cesena, and he was in many ways worse.
This dispute had still not been resolved—indeed, there were at one
point *three* popes—and the papacy was also now entering its famous
debauched Renaissance era: in 1413, the 'antipope'—that is, a pope
not recognized by the Church—John XXIII had been deposed on
charges of 'piracy, murder, rape, sodomy, and incest,' but the historian Edmund Gibbon said the 'most scandalous' charges were
suppressed. John was eventually imprisoned, although freed after
the powerful Medici family paid off his jailors.

Although rather unsympathetic a figure, Henry had the strong
leadership skills that were necessary at the time. Two northern land-
owners who were in a long-running dispute with each other were
brought before him as he was about to dine and told that unless they
had ended their argument and found a solution before he had finished his oysters, they would both be hanged. They agreed.

Two years into his reign, Henry V reignited the war with France;
the second half of the Hundred Years' War was as violent, brutal,

and criminal as the first, although Henry was stricter with his men than Edward III had been, probably because he was a religious fanatic while Edward was just an upper-class hooligan who loved fighting. So soldiers were not to rape women or steal from priests or churches; in 1415, one man was caught with a container for consecrated bread and immediately hanged by the king.[15] Before setting sail, the pious ruler set up two monasteries, in Sheen and Syon on the River Thames, and he also granted Richard II a proper state funeral. The language of the common English soldier was not so pious; during this period, the French called them Goddams because of their swearing.

There was one useful side effect to this war: Henry's father had been the first king since 1066 to speak English as a first language, and Henry V was the first to use it for business, and his frequent letters on the progress of the war on the continent are seen by some experts as helping to create Standard English.[16] Henry, in fact, was such a xenophobe that he claimed he didn't know French and refused to use it in council,[17] even though the war was being fought over his claim to the French throne, which could only be justified by demonstrating his French blood.

French divisions

England is a quarter the size of France and at the time its population was less than a fifth, but it was able to invade its larger neighbor because it was wracked by extreme division, largely caused by the insanity of Charles VI. King Charles had come to the throne aged just twelve in 1380, and things were going pretty well until one day on campaign, in August 1392, he suddenly became psychotic, killing five people with a lance in an hour-long episode before being overpowered. It had been a hot day and Charles was leading an army through the countryside near Le Mans in the west of the country. The king was in a stressed state and there had been a recent assassination attempt against one of his friends, and then a local lunatic shouted at him that he faced treachery from unknown persons within his ranks. Then a lance dropped, making a clanging sound; it was all too much for him, and after that he went in and out of insanity.

The French court had by this stage already began sliding into a weird sort of debauchery, with increasingly depraved and sinister figures hanging around, among them Charles's German wife Isabeau, a grasping sex maniac who had a succession of lovers.[18]

It had been a terrible time. France had suffered almost four decades of war from 1340 on, and had been riddled with roving bands of 'Free Companies,' mostly English mercenary armies that controlled large swathes of the country and committed various atrocities. On top of this there was the plague and the rural insurrection known as the Jacquerie, in which French peasants took delight in killing nobles (and vice versa).

During periods of insanity, Charles foamed at the mouth and refused to wash (and so became covered with sores and his own feces, and infested with vermin). He would eat from the floor, and became obsessed with the idea that he was made of glass and would shatter if touched, screaming that he felt a thousand iron spikes ripping into his flesh. King Charles's servants at the Hôtel Saint-Pol, the royal residence in Paris, eventually walled up the palace doors to stop him from escaping, as he ran around wildly.

People thought his condition was caused by wet or melancholic humor—black bile as it was called—one of the four 'humors' identified by Greek physicians that was still medical consensus at the time. Historical diagnosis is a sketchy business, but some historians believe Charles suffered from schizophrenia, which runs in families; Charles's mother Jeanne de Bourbon had also suffered a nervous breakdown and several other family members were highly neurotic.

As a result, the court divided into two rival factions led by, on one hand, the king's brother Louis de Valois, Duke of Orléans and on the other, Philippe the Bold, Duke of Burgundy, a cousin. Their respective power depended on how insane the king was at the time. When the king was deranged, the country was ruled by his cousin Burgundy, who siphoned off up to one-sixth of the annual revenue to the treasury of his own region (which included not just the area of eastern France famous for red wine, but also his wife's lands in what is now Belgium and southern Holland). When Charles was sane, his brother Orléans was running things, 'no less of a bloodsucker than his uncle Philippe.'[19] Orléans was married to the daughter of Gian, Duke of Milan, and hoped to use French money in order to buy the dukedom of the city-state, one of Italy's richest. The taxes he imposed made him even more unpopular than his rival, and he was also suspected of practicing magic.

People began to divide into factions, led by Philippe's son Jean the Fearless, who was 'singularly ugly, with an excessively long nose, an undershot jaw, and a crooked mouth' and was 'harsh, cynical, crafty, imperious, gloomy, and a killjoy.'[20] The Orléanists chose a badge of a wooden club to signify Louis beating down his opponents, so Jean's Burgundians adopted a carpenter's plane to signify cutting the club in half. The two sides hated each other, clearly.

On November 20, 1407, Jean and Louis took Holy Communion together. Three days later, on Jean's instructions, Louis was ambushed after visiting the Queen and his hand was chopped off and brains scattered on the road. Jean the Fearless cried at the funeral of his cousin, saying 'never was a more treacherous murder' committed, but just two days later, suspecting he was to be caught out, he owned up and told his uncle 'I did it; the Devil tempted me.' Not the greatest master criminal, he fled to Flanders. Louis's eldest son, Charles, therefore, went into alliance with his father-in-law Bernard, Count of Armagnac, and the two groups became known as the Burgundians and Armagnacs, a suitably French-sounding civil war in which both sides are also the names of alcoholic drinks.

As the conflict escalated, Henry of Monmouth, still just a prince, decided to get involved, and in 1411 led a group of 1,200

Englishmen to help the Burgundians at St. Cloud in a battle against some *ecorcheurs*—flayers, mercenaries known for their cruelty—allied to the Armagnacs. Unfortunately, this seems to have given him a taste for it, and so upon becoming king, Henry V signed a treaty with the Armagnacs, in which his lordship was recognized over the regions of Poitou, Angouleme, and Perigord, areas just north of the English province of Gascony. However, in 1415, Henry also insisted on having Normandy, Maine, Anjou, Brittany, and Touraine, the lands that had constituted the empire of Henry II some two and a half centuries previously; when it was refused, as it inevitably would be, he launched an invasion.

Charles VI had helped the future Henry IV by letting him stay in Paris, but the French soon turned against the Lancastrians who they claimed to be illegitimate and whose ambassadors they snubbed with typical Gallic distain. After Henry claimed the throne of France, in March 1415 the French king supposedly sent him a gift of tennis balls, offering that since he was a youngster, he could have 'little balls to play with and soft cushions to lie upon, until he had grown manly strength later on.' Guaranteed to upset the ego of a twenty-four-year-old man, the rebuff was saying that not only was he not the rightful king of France, but he wasn't the rightful king of England either.

There was little enthusiasm in England for a war, which was very much a one-man crusade. As historian Ian Mortimer put it, 'Most of his fellow commanders considered his judgement suspect, if not plain wrong. Nevertheless, they followed him. They did so on account of his remarkable leadership skills, his pious devotion to God, and because Henry gave them little choice: as the chronicler Jean de Waurin noted, even a whiff of dissent caused him to have men executed.'[21] In November 1414, Parliament voted for a fresh tax to raise money for Henry's pet war, but it wasn't enough, so commissioners were dispatched to find more and they tried to get cash wherever they could. In 1417, every goose in southern England had to give six feathers for use in arrows.[22]

However, before battle could begin there came the Southampton Plot of August 1415, a conspiracy to kill the king and have him replaced with his cousin Edmund Mortimer. The ringleaders were Thomas Grey—who sat on the King's Council, and whose son was betrothed to the four-year-old daughter of Edmund Mortimer's sister Anne—and the Earl of Cambridge, the king's cousin. However, Mortimer was a bit scared of the idea and informed Henry; Cambridge, Grey, and three others were beheaded. Mortimer did this despite the fact that the king had just fined him ten thousand marks—similar to around five million dollars or so today—for marrying his wife Anne without his permission, which was all part of the king's scheme to raise as much money as possible. Cambridge, whose wife Anne had died four years earlier, left two young children as orphans, Isabel, six, and three-year-old Richard. Richard of York, as he would become after his uncle Edward of Langley's death on the battlefield, would be the key player in the future civil war.

God for Harry, England, and Saint George

On August 14, 1415, Henry landed near Harfleur in Normandy along with fifteen thousand troops, the plan being to take control of the river. He laid siege on the 17th, but the town was well provisioned, and to make matters worse its marshy estuary was full of fever-carrying insects. On top of malaria, many perished from food poisoning after eating fruit, getting 'the bloody flux,' (as dysentery was called), or after drinking bad wine and cider; a third of Henry's army died before Harfleur eventually fell on September 22. However, the siege became part of English popular culture, as it was here that William Shakespeare has the king urging his men to go 'once more onto the breach,' one of the bard's most famous lines.

Henry wanted to march to Gascony, which was still in the hands of the English, but his advisers said this would be impossible so instead he decided to head northeast to Calais using the traditional English war tactic of the *chevauchée*, which originally meant a sort of countryside jaunt, but came to denote a rampaging orgy of murder and theft aimed at forcing the opposing king to come out and fight. This was Edward III's favored method, although the French usually just waited until the English ran out of food or started dying of dysentery.

This time it worked, and the French army caught up with the English outside the village of Maisoncelle, although for some reason the battle came to be known by the further-away town of Azincourt, or Agincourt in English.

Shakespeare shows the king walking around camp on the eve of battle, engaging in small talk with ordinary soldiers, giving them 'a little touch of Harry in the night.' In reality, lighthearted banter was one thing he definitely didn't go in for and Henry banned men from speaking on the night before in case there was defeatist talk, on pain of mutilation. On top of this, the king slept near the village of Blangy, under cover, while his men had to rough it out in the open in drenching rain, 'the luckier finding some wretched shelter beneath trees or bushes.'

Indeed, Henry thought he'd lose Agincourt and tried to do a deal to get free passage to Calais in return for Harfleur, but the French said no. The English were outnumbered four or five-to-one, so it must have felt fairly hopeless.

In 1356, the English under the 'Black Prince' Edward of Woodstock had won a spectacular victory at Poitiers, where they were even more outnumbered because their lethal and disciplined archers were more effective than the French cavalry. The cavalry had been a pillar of medieval society because it meant power lay with the aristocrats who could afford the armor, but the whole culture of chivalry, while it did promote clemency and rules about fighting, also encouraged people to show off and try to win glory in battle. This was no match for disciplined armies, and Agincourt further reinforced this lesson.

The French hadn't selected a battleground where their numerical superiority would help but were instead forced to stand in three rows with little room for maneuvering. There was no one in charge of tactics: the nobles all competed to be in the front line and archers were placed behind, where they were useless. Their Constable Charles d'Albret had before the battle rejected an offer of six thousand crossbowmen from Paris's citizen militia and instead was given heavier plate armor, which increased fatigue and reduced mobility.

The French cavalry charged forward and were struck by arrows and wooden stakes laid by the English beforehand. One theory is that Henry's battle plan, of laying down sharpened stakes, had been thought up by Frenchman Marshal Boucicaut and previously used against the Turks, and that the Duke of York had read about it and suggested it to his cousin.

The French were also weighed down by the muddy ground, and lots of men actually drowned in the battle; many more died as a result of suffocation, crushed under the weight of men and armor. Others were killed with 'swords, hatchets, mallets, axes, falcon-beaks and other weapons.' The English account in the *Gesta Henrici* says: 'For when some of them, killed when battle was first joined, fall at the front, so great was the undisciplined violence and pressure of the mass of men behind them that the living fell on top of the dead, and others falling on top of the living were killed as well.'

Right in the thick of things, enjoying every minute of it, was King Henry. At one point, the Duke of Alençon beat the king to his knees and hacked a floret from his crown; but the Duke of Alençon was soon surrounded by men and offered his gloves in surrender, but was 'cut down by a berserk English knight' who staved his head in. Another aristocrat, the Duke of Brabant, was killed because he'd rushed into battle without all his armor, and so the English thought he was just a herald and killed him.

The Duke of York, brother of one of the Southampton plotters, managed to redeem the family name by dying in battle, although it wasn't actually a very heroic death; York was forty-five and very fat and, after falling over, was suffocated by bodies falling on top of him and then had a heart attack. He had not been scratched during the fight, but even so, by his death it meant his brother's son Richard was able to inherit the title of York. The armor of this period was extremely heavy and it was not unheard of for men to die of heart failure during battles inside their 'cocoons.' (It was also impossible to get up once one had fallen down, and so pages had to lift their lords off the ground as otherwise they were helpless.)

There is a popular myth that before the battle the French said they would cut off the index and forefingers of every English archer, in order that the world's greatest bowmen could not trouble them again; so when victory came, they stuck two fingers up at the French, and that is why the V-sign is a popular rude gesture in England. Unfortunately, like most good stories, it's not true, or at least there is no evidence for it, and the V-sign, beloved by British street urchins with poor dentistry, probably came about much later.

Meanwhile, the English committed what many in France regard as a terrible war crime. While the battle was still raging, the local lord, Ysambart d'Azincourt, had come down with some six hundred locals to attack the English baggage carts, which were full of plunder. Fearing he was to be attacked and their fifteen hundred French prisoners would overwhelm them, Henry ordered his men to kill them. The aristocratic soldiers refused to do this, whether out of greed or compassion (as their prisoners were worth money), so he got two hundred of the lowest grade men to commit the atrocity, and ordered the execution of anyone who refused.

In the entire battle, the English lost no more than three hundred men, by some estimates as few as 120, including just ten or so nobles; in contrast, hundreds of French aristocrats were killed, as well as between seven to ten thousand of the common French soldiers, the *gent d'armes*, or men at arms (which is where they get *gendarme*, the term for police, French police still being of a somewhat military and no-nonsense nature).

After the battle, Henry did not bother to bury the English dead, the bodies just being thrown in a barn and burned, and when the soldiers reached Calais they were forced to camp outside the town and were not given food or shelter; many had to hand over prisoners in exchanges. Three years later, and some still hadn't been paid.

Afterwards, he went on a seven-year rampage through France. In 1417 at Rouen, the English king deliberately starved to death all the inhabitants, another break with the traditional rules of war. In November that year when Caen fell, Henry had eighteen hundred men and boys put to death. When a Dominican friar asked him how he could do such a thing, the king replied, sounding utterly demented: 'I am the scourge of God sent to punish the people of God for their sins.'

Henry committed what would today be called war crimes on a number of occasions, at Rouen, Caen, Pontoise, Melun, Rougemont, and Meaux; even by the standards of the day he was considered to have broken basic rules of conflict. On September 4, 1417, there was horrific violence in Caen after the city fell, and the English king only ordered an end to the slaughter after he 'saw a baby sucking at the breast of its headless mother,' which even for him was a bit much.[23] Strangely, none of this appeared in the Shakespeare play. In June 1418, Henry took Louviers on the Seine, and when it surrendered he hanged eight gunners for firing at his tent (it was claimed he had them crucified, but that seems unlikely for such a devout Christian).

Henry V took Caen because its citizens couldn't bring themselves to demolish two old abbeys, built by William the Conqueror, which were just outside the walls; the English therefore seized them and they were used as artillery platforms. Most continental cities had defensive walls against besieging armies, called 'bulwarks,' or 'boulevards' (the word originally meaning artillery ramparts and only later being applied to the pretty, tree-lined avenues that replaced them).[24] That's why even very old continental cities usually have grand boulevards around the old town, while old English cities are higgledy-piggledy, as they didn't need bulwarks because the sea protected them from marauding armies.

Then in 1418–1419 came Rouen, downstream on the River Seine, where the English king deliberately starved to death all the inhabitants. The city was defended by twenty-two thousand men, but the siege would show the utter ruthlessness of the English king. When Henry hanged prisoners in front of the walls, the Norman captain of the crossbowmen, Alain Blanchard, hanged Englishmen from the ramparts with dead dogs around their necks, and the vicar-general of Rouen excommunicated Henry from within the walls.

By October, the inhabitants of the Norman capital were eating horseflesh. Some twelve thousand elderly people and nursing mothers—useless mouths to feed—were driven out, expecting to be allowed to pass the English lines, but to their horror Henry refused to let them through and they died there in the ditch. Even the English troops felt sorry for them.

Rouen surrendered on January 19, 1419, and upon entering, Henry kissed each of the forty-two crosses carried by clergymen after attending a Mass of thanksgiving at the church of Saint-Maclou. The cleric who had excommunicated Henry would spend five years in chains; Blanchard was hanged straight away. The survivors 'looked like funeral effigies, deaths from hunger continuing for days despite the arrival of food carts.'[25] The city was sacked, and at least two thousand were killed.

Henry went on to sack Argentan, Falaise, and Cherbourg during his rampage across northwest France. At the Siege of Montereau, he again hanged prisoners in front of the town. At Melun, the commander, Arnaud de Barbazan, only escaped the rope under the laws of chivalry: they had crossed swords under the siege-mines beneath the walls and were therefore brothers-in-arms. He was put in a cage, but Henry strung up twenty Scottish prisoners.

The slightest insult could provoke him; the king had Jean de Villiers, marshal of France, arrested for looking at him in the face when answering a question—and he was an ally. The flip side of this was a fearsomely magnetic personality, so that in May 1418 a clergyman, St. Vincent Ferrer, came to Caen saying Henry was the 'scourge of God,' but after a personal meeting left saying he now thought Henry's 'quarrel is so just and true that undoubtedly God is and shall be his aid[e] in these wars.' What the king said to the man will remain a mystery.

Despite the horror of the English invasion, the French court was unable to act because it was so ridden with factions, and things continued to get worse. Two dauphins—heirs to the French throne—died in succession, eighteen-year-old Louis in December 1415, of dysentery, and his brother Jean in April 1417, also then eighteen, either of an abscess or of poisoning (poisoning was always a possibility in the French court). This left just one son left, Charles, 'a hapless fourteen-year-old' whose own mother had pronounced him illegitimate.'[26] The younger Charles was, although not mad, highly neurotic and had a terrible fear that if he walked into a house it would fall down on him, after such a horror did happen in La Rochelle (it was much easier to be neurotic at a time when utterly horrific things actually did occur more often). Father and son, despite sharing a madness, fell out, leaving Henry in a stronger position.

The French court had also reached new depths of seediness, so when the Church authorities raided the castle of one courtier, Gilles de Rais, they found the remains of over fifty children; Rais, a serial killer before the concept existed, murdered as many as 140 victims; that's when he wasn't spending his vast fortune on amateur stage productions in his chateau. He was executed in 1440, aged thirty-five, but he became immortalized by the French folktale, *Bluebeard*, which was first published in Paris in 1697.

By the summer of 1419, France was terrified of the English scourge but the court was crippled by its internal hatreds, the two factions as divided as ever. On September 10, the Burgundians and

Armangacs had held a peace meeting at the bridge at Montereau, thirty-five miles outside Paris, which didn't go entirely well. The two sides talked, voices were raised, insults were thrown, and then the dauphin's followers attacked Jean the Fearless 'as he knelt in homage before the new dauphin' and 'dashed him down stark dead to the ground.' It was what diplomats would today call a 'firm and frank exchange of views.'

The head ended up being kept by monks in Dijon as a curio/ conversation piece.

One of those involved in negotiations between the two French factions was a poet, Georges Chastellain, whose phrase rather sums up the mood of the time: 'I, man of sadness, born in an eclipse of darkness amid fogs of lamentation.'

It was said afterward that the English entered France through the hole in the Duke of Burgundy's skull, as there could be no peace between the two French factions now. Jean's successor, Duke Philippe the Good, allied formally with Henry and offered him the crown. At Troyes on May 21, 1420, peace was made, providing for the marriage between the English king and Catherine of Valois, the daughter of Charles VI. Queen Isabeau had sided with Philippe, whose father had been killed by her son's soldiers, disavowing her son's claim, while King Charles was now so mad that he did not even know who Henry was when he met him.

Afterward, the English king took his new wife on honeymoon— while besieging the city of Sens. She must have been charmed. When King Henry rode into Paris, spending twelve days over Christmas at the Louvre, the city was in such a state of starvation that houses were pulled down for firewood and wolves could be seen swimming the Seine to eat corpses lying in the street. That month, Catherine's brother Charles was formally disinherited, and on February 1 she set sail for England to prepare for her coronation. Three weeks later, she was crowned at Westminster Abbey, attended by most of the realm's nobility, among them the Scottish king James, who had been kidnapped by the English fourteen years earlier and was still a prisoner.

The House of Lancaster was triumphant, but its greatest victory contained the seeds of its downfall. Henry soon alienated many Burgundians, including the marshal of France, who did not like being berated for looking at him. Then, in April 1421, Henry's brother Thomas, Duke of Clarence, was killed in idiotic fashion. While in camp, he had been informed of an Armagnac army nearby and his advisers told him to wait until the archers arrived, but he scoffed: 'If you are afraid, go home and keep the churchyard.' He set off with only fifteen hundred men at arms, and when he saw the enemy, he charged uphill even though they outnumbered him two to one and they were on boggy ground. Clarence was easily identified by his coronet and killed.

Soon Catherine was pregnant, but before his son's birth, Henry V had been told by a soothsayer (conveniently) that 'Henry of Windsor shall long reign and lose all' and warned his wife not to give birth at Windsor Castle, but while he was out on campaign she ignored his advice and a son, Henry, was born in December. Ever the devout Christian, when his wife went into labor, Henry sent a messenger to ride sixty miles to collect Christ's foreskin from Coulombs, near Chartres, as good luck (Coulombs is one of seventeen churches across Europe to have claimed to own Jesus's foreskin).

The following May, Henry V marched on to the city of Meaux, where along the way he beheaded a trumpeter called Orace for mocking him. However, near the town he contracted the bloody flux and died in August. A month later, the same fate fell to the King of France. Before he perished, Henry V paid for twenty thousand Masses to be said for his soul, but toward the end witnesses reported that he seemed to be talking to evil spirits, apparently no longer sure God was pleased with his life's work.

Charles's end was in many ways a release for him, while that of Henry V was no doubt one for many others. Certainly, getting killed was a good career move, as he'd already upset quite a few people and he was only unassailably popular because he kept on winning against the odds, and that couldn't last forever. Afterwards, the war would peter out—and the soothsayer's prophecy would turn out to be true.

CHAPTER THREE

Foul Fiend of France and Hag of All Despite

Henry's death had left his joint kingdom in crisis from the start, especially as the new king of France and England was just nine months old, and so had it rather stacked against him.

If the raising of children into royalty today can seem cruel with the relentless glare of publicity, it was nothing compared to the stresses on a medieval monarch brought up on the throne, with various family members literally trying to kill one another. To make things worse, Henry VI, as well as gaining the crowns of both England and France, had also inherited his French grandfather's serious mental illness. The new king was the polar opposite of his father, a deeply tragic, childlike figure who got upset by the sight of blood or nudity.

After the old king's death, one surviving brother, John, Duke of Bedford, was declared regent of France while the youngest Humphrey, the Duke of Gloucester, became lord protector of England. Gloucester was also appointed *tutela* to Henry VI, an old Roman word that meant guardian, during the king's minority, and while he wanted to be made regent of England, this was blocked by his many opponents at home; instead Parliament made him 'defender of the kingdom of England and the English church and principal councillor of the lord King.' It was a grand title, but his authority was limited, and only above others so long as his brother Bedford was away in France.

Gloucester was arrogant and ruthless; in 1428, he had cast aside his wife Jacqueline of Hainault, having the marriage annulled so he could pursue Eleanor Cobham, one of her ladies-in-waiting. Bedford, in contrast, was perhaps the only Englishman over the course of the 115-year-long conflict to be not completely hated by the French. On top of many other things, he did his best to help French people against the *ecorcheurs*, or flayers, highwaymen who had arisen out of the war and would skin their victims alive. Bedford had married the Duke of Burgundy's sister Anne for political reasons, and even though she was 'as plain as an owl,' it became a happy marriage.

Two years after Henry's death, the English scored perhaps an even bigger victory at Verneuil on August 17, 1424. The disinherited 'Charles VII' of France, officially referred to by the English as 'he who calls himself the dauphin,' raised an army, a mix of French, Scots, Spanish, and Lombards from northern Italy, who were the best armed and most terrifying soldiers in Europe. Against them was an English force led by Bedford, alongside Thomas Montacute, Earl of Salisbury, who, at thirty-six, was one of the most famous soldiers in Christendom. The battle began with a cavalry charge by the Lombard mercenaries, and at one point the English standard fell, but a Norman knight went into the French lines and retrieved it.

The day ended with some seven thousand French and Scots lying dead, among them the earls of Buchan and Archibald Douglas, the same Douglas who had been captured by the Percys; afterwards he was nicknamed 'Tyneman,' Scottish for 'loser,' not the best epitaph. Scottish troops had become a big presence in France, but their allies found them to be a handful and one French military leader suggested that although the battle was a disaster, it was offset by being rid of the Scots, 'whose insolence was intolerable' and who were referred to as 'drunken, mutton-eating fools.'[27] The French still hated each other as well: the Paris *Bourgeois*, a chronicle of the time, describes the crimes of the Armagnacs as 'worse than Saracens' or 'unchained devils.' Afterward, Bedford, who had led from the front with a poleax, was cheered upon his return to Paris.

However, it all went downhill for the English after that. There was a Norman resistance movement, which overlapped with a certain level of criminal brigandage that always springs up in such circumstances. The English had mass-produced posters showing Henry VI's descent from the kings of France, but the one at Notre-Dame Cathedral was vandalized by a priest. Although conquerors and occupiers, the English banned their soldiers from calling the enemy 'Frenchmen,' and could only refer to them as 'Armagnacs,' the name of the anti-English faction, in a futile attempt to maintain some sort of legitimacy for Henry VI's rule.

There was also factional conflict in London, and, in 1425, a personal feud erupted between Humphrey and his uncle, Henry Beaufort, bishop of Winchester. Beaufort was Henry IV's half brother, the second son of John of Gaunt by his mistress-turned-third wife Katherine Swynford. The Beauforts were originally born out of wedlock but had been legitimized by Henry IV—although on the condition none could become king—and would play a key role in the conflict to come. Henry IV, once in power, had made his brother Lord Chancellor in 1403, but Beaufort later sided with his nephew, the future Henry V, against the king. Although a churchman, he fathered at least one illegitimate daughter, and now aged fifty, was also very wealthy and had helped to keep the Crown going with loans; however, he wasn't popular with the Londoners and a mob threatened to dunk the bishop in a pond if they found him.

The dispute had begun after Humphrey had led a foolhardy military adventure into Hainault in what is now Belgium in pursuit of his wife's claim there, lands that were now occupied by her first husband John of Brabant, who was supported by the Duke of Burgundy. Humphrey brought over five thousand men, which undermined Bedford—who was the duke's brother-in-law—thus almost destroying theAnglo-Burgundian alliance. Humphrey was supported by the Earl of Salisbury out of spite, because Philippe of Burgundy, a notorious womanizer with thirty mistresses, had made a pass at his nineteen-year-old wife. It was followed by an outbreak of anti-Flemish rioting in London.

Beaufort had gathered an army to bring order to the city, which Gloucester thought was an attempt to attack him and take over, and the tension was defused by Henry Chichelel, archbishop of Canterbury, as well as the king's cousin Pedro, Prince of Portugal, who just happened to be staying as a guest. Over the course of a tense day, they each helped send messages between the two camps, eight times in total, with offers of a truce. However, the conflict between the cardinal and Duke Humphrey escalated so much that when Parliament met at Leicester in 1426, it became known as the Parliament of Bats, as everyone turned up armed.

In 1428, the English besieged Orléans, south of France, where, on October 27, their commander Salisbury was mortally wounded by debris from a stone cannonball fired from across the river. Half his face was blown off. A lengthy siege followed, now led by William de la Pole, the thirty-two-year-old Earl of Suffolk, only broken for Christmas Day when Suffolk sent some figs to the French leader Jean, 'the Bastard of Orléans' (it was meant as a term of affection) and received a fur coat in exchange. The city lent the besiegers an orchestra to entertain them.

However, the English were completely unprepared for what happened next, for in 1428 a 'certain witch of France,' as Bedford put it, had 'succeeded by enchantments' in defeating them.

Joan of Arc

English rule in France wasn't a total festival of plunder and drunkenness. The Duke of Bedford was a Renaissance man and his numerous houses, in Paris, Rouen, and elsewhere contained a fine collection of artworks, books, and treasures. The English also founded universities at Caen and Poitiers in 1431, while back home All Souls College, Oxford, was opened in 1438. This period also saw the first named written music (and Henry V probably wrote pieces himself). The English occupation of Paris in the 1420s and 1430s led to a flowering of music, and John Dunstaple, the Duke of Bedford's household musician, set the fashion in France. *Contenance Angloise*, or English manner, was a musical style at the time, sort of like the British Invasion of the 1960s if the Beatles and Rolling Stones had come to America with heavily armed bands of mercenaries.

Across Europe, universities sprung up in the early fifteenth century at Louvain, Glasgow, Basle, Freiburg, St. Andrews, Leipzig, Rostock, and Catania. England was relatively backwards, but the Italian humanist Poggio spent three years there at the invitation of Bishop Beaufort, and Humphrey, Duke of Gloucester invited Italian humanists such as Tito Livio Frulovisi, who was commissioned to write a life of Henry V. By the mid-fifteenth century, Englishmen were going to Italy to learn from the classical scholars.

England also imported French artists, such as Charles of Orléans, who translated French romantic poetry into English— since the English had held him prisoner for twenty-one years, he certainly had time on his hands. Charles had been captured at Agincourt, and during his time in captivity he became the writer of the first Valentine's Day poem.

The term 'Middle Ages' was first used in 1469 by a bishop, Giovanni Andrea, who was obsessed with Greece and Rome and thought Europeans were returning to it, and away from the darkness of the *media tempesta*. The word 'Renaissance' was first coined by the fourteenth century Italian poet Petrarch, and the concept can be specifically dated to 1341 when the King of Naples placed a laurel wreath on Petrarch's head in an elaborate ceremony, symbolizing a sort of rebirth of ancient Rome. Later, in the 1490s, the French had invaded Italy, one of the unintended consequences being they came back with lots of ideas about philosophy, science, art, and mathematics; in return, they gave the Italians syphilis.[28]

However the idea of the Middle Ages divides academics, and some take the view of historian Brian Stock that: 'The Renaissance invented the Middle Ages in order to define itself; the Enlightenment perpetuated them in order to admire itself; and the Romantics revived them in order to escape from themselves. In their wildest ramifications "the Middle Ages" thus constitute one of the most prevalent cultural myths of the modern world.' Much of the most horrific torture and cruelty we think of typically 'medieval' actually occurred in the early modern period.

Among the new renaissance men was Richard Beauchamp, the Earl of Warwick, one of the best and most chivalrous of English soldiers of the Hundred Years' War. Beauchamp was Henry VI's tutor, had been all around Europe and was given the honorific title 'Father of Courtesy' by the Holy Roman Emperor Sigismund because of his learning. He also ended up burning to death France's patron saint, Joan of Arc.

The 'Pucelle,' or Maid, had first appeared in February 1428: Jehanne d'Arc, as she was later known, was aged just seventeen and illiterate, and came from Domremy in Lorraine in northeast France. Although dismissed as a simple peasant, her father was a landowner with fifty acres, and prominent in their town on the border with Champagne; Domremy had been besieged by the Anglo-Burgundian army so there was a general patriotic mood there.

Joan had been receiving divine voices since she was thirteen, and claimed to have been visited by the saints Michael, Margaret, and Catherine, all figures depicted carrying swords and who are popular among soldiers; Margaret and Catherine were both martyred for refusing to marry pagans while Michael was associated with fighting. At the age of sixteen, she decided to act on the voices and told her mother she was off to see her cousin and then ran away, like many teenage girls, except most don't do so to lead national wars of liberation. Joan went to the local nobleman, Robert de Baudricourt, and told him that she had been sent by God to save France. He told his servants to beat 'the mad girl,' the modish treatment at the time for people with mental health issues.

However, locals began hearing about Joan and getting behind her, and luckily there was a popular local prophecy made by a mystic called Marie d'Avignon in which it was said a 'virgin girl from the borders of Lorraine' would save France. Eventually, de Baudricourt, tired of her pleading and happy to get her as far away from him as possible, gave Joan an armed escort to meet Charles, the dauphin, who was almost four hundred miles away in Chinon.

The skeptical dauphin kept her waiting outside Chinon's walls, and as she walked into the town a soldier mocked her, saying 'By God, let me have her one night, and she won't be a virgin any more [*sic*]' to which she replied, 'It might be dangerous to take the Lord's name in vain when you're so close to death.' He later fell in the moat and died, which Joan's supporters took great satisfaction in recounting, a sign then of God's support, although even the most strident feminist today would probably say it was a bit harsh.

Contemporary politician Jean de Waurin wrote of Joan's arrival that: 'At court, they thought she was a deluded lunatic, because she boasted of being able to accomplish tasks so difficult that the great princes thought them impossible.' Charles tried to trick Joan by having a fake dauphin greet her, but she picked out the right man instead. The dauphin's associates interrogated her and in the end thought that, as they were getting hammered, there was little to lose—for them if not her—if she led an army out. First Joan was given a virginity test—had she not being pious, then her religious visions would have been obviously fraudulent—and after passing she was given armor and put in charge of four thousand men.

Rather than being sectioned, Joan quickly became a hero to the French despite her sex, and soldiers began flocking to her. She would even live with the troops and had no qualms about undressing in front of them, one veteran describing her 'beautiful' breasts, which left him strangely unaroused because she was so holy, which is always a bit of a passion killer, even for a sex-starved medieval Frenchman.

Soon she rode to Orléans on a white horse, with an army of several thousand soldiers and some priests, and carrying a sword that some people believed belonged to Charles Martel, the Frankish warrior who had repelled the Arabs at the Battle of Tours in 732. When Joan and her army arrived in the city, the English ran away, thinking her a witch, dumping their cannons and heavy weapons in their haste to escape.

Joan wrote to the dauphin telling him she'd have him crowned at the cathedral in Reims, the traditional coronation site of the kings of France, and to its citizens telling them to prepare for a coronation. At the time, this sounded like a totally insane thing to say. Likewise were the demands she made of the English, in one letter compelling them to 'Restore to the Maid, who is sent here by God, the king of heaven, the keys of all the fine towns that you have taken and violated in France.' Her language was 'rambling and repetitive, looping in circles, veering from third person to first and back again.'[29] One leading English commander suggested that Joan was a 'trollop' who should go back to herding cattle.[30]

The Burgundians hoped to counter Joan's popularity with their own resident fanatic, a friar in Troyes called Brother Richard. For ten days in April that year, Brother Richard had preached about the coming of the Antichrist to thousands of people, scaring them so much with his warnings of hellfire that the townspeople made huge bonfires of playing cards, dice, chessboards, 'and every kind of covetous game that can give rise to anger and swearing'; women even threw expensive headdresses into the flames. However, while the city elders were strongly opposed to the Armagnacs, Brother Richard shocked them and the English by giving Joan his support.

Bedford sent a message to the people of Paris in which he said the so-called dauphin was exploiting the ignorant aided by two 'superstitious and reprobate characters,' both 'abominable in the sight of God,' one 'a sluttish woman of ill repute, dressed as a man and dissolute in her conduct' and the other 'an apostate and seditious friar.' (Sluttish that is, in the older sense, of being slovenly.)

Then on June 18, 1429, at the Battle at Patay, the French destroyed an English force, with two thousand men killed and only one English captain, John Fastolf, surviving. On July 16, Charles entered Reims and the following day was crowned at the ancient coronation site of the kings of France, where his ancestor Clovis had converted the Franks to Christianity in the fifth century. It wasn't a perfect coronation—the English had all of the regalia of Charlemagne at Saint-Denis, but they made use with a substitute crown and sword, as well as sacred oil, helpfully collected by serial killer Gilles de Rais and three others.'[31] At Charles's side was Joan, an astonishing rise for an illiterate farmhand; but as with any media-led flavor of the month, however, her downfall would be almost as swift, with those who previously hailed her now jumping off the bandwagon.

Charles now signed a truce with the Burgundians, but Joan publicly announced that while she was happy with the peace, she wasn't sure if she would keep it. Joan then attacked occupied Paris and demanded of the English: 'Surrender to us quickly, in the name of Jesus! For if you do not surrender before nightfall, we will come in there by force, whether you like it or not, and you will be put to death without mercy.' The reply came, in rather less elevated language: 'Shall we, you bloody tart?' This was followed by a crossbow bolt that hit her thigh, while her standard bearer beside her was killed with a shot between his eyes. Joan had to be carried away with her leg bleeding, angry that she was being taken from the fight.

Then, when she went to Soissons, where the townspeople weren't friendly toward the French army on account of their soldiers' previous behavior there, she wasn't allowed in. Many deserted her and her power seemed to be waning. Joan then attacked Compiègne, but on May 23, 1430, was captured by an archer in the pay of the Burgundians. By now, the archbishop of Reims, previously sympathetic, washed his hands of the Maid, saying they'd found a new messenger of God, a shepherd boy in the Languedoc. She was yesterday's news.

Many French people were indeed horrified by Joan. A chronicle written between 1405 and 1449, called *Journal d'un Bourgeois de Paris*, talks of the 'enormous sins that she did commit, and cause to be committed, and how she caused ordinary people to commit idolatry because by her false hypocrisy.' And the anonymous writer of the *Journal* was no foreign stooge, and said of the English that they 'burn those they can't ransom, rape nuns, and eat meat on a Friday' and 'the English, by nature, always want to fight their neighbors for no reason, which is why they always die badly.'

The Church was increasingly hostile toward Joan, and the grand inquisitor of France, Martin Billori, demanded of the Burgundians that they hand her over for trial because she had caused the 'perdition of several simple Christians.' The Duke of Bedford had lost Orléans because of Joan, and the Maid had also sent him insulting letters, saying he would 'be hearing from the Virgin, and the meeting will cause you much pain,' so she had not charmed him. Joan also angered the English by insisting the saints spoke French and not English; she was the 'Foul fiend of France and hag of all despite,' as Shakespeare has them saying. So, Bedford agreed to buy her off the Burgundians for 10 percent of English France's annual income, or ten thousand livre tournois.

In the shambolic, one-sided trial that followed, she was prosecuted by Archbishop Cauchon of Rouen, with the main judge assisted by Jean le Maitre, the 'Vicar to the Inquisitor of Heretical Perversity,' who, as his title suggests, was not a wet liberal.

Among the seventy charges against her were those of witchcraft, blasphemy, fighting a battle on a Sunday, and wearing men's clothes. Many of these carried the death sentence, although the cross-dressing was, strangely, especially serious. Joan wore her pants and tunic 'firmly laced and tied together,' which was considered an abomination, and she refused to change them for a skirt in case she got assaulted by prison guards, although some Englishmen seemed to be scared she was a devil and so didn't touch her.

With the trial swiftly concluded, she was taken to the town square at Rouen on May 30, 1341, where a French mob jeered at her as she was burned to death, still only nineteen; as she died, an English soldier put two sticks together to give her an improvised cross. Afterward, her charred body was exposed to show she was indeed female, before it was properly burned to discourage it from becoming a shrine. As the French used to joke, Joan is 'the only thing the English have ever cooked properly.'[32]

Fashions change, however, and within a generation the Witch of Orléans was popular again, since country people kept on talking about her. While the authorities had tried to stop pilgrimages to Rouen and Orléans in honor of the Maid, they were fighting a losing battle. By this stage, France had won the war and so her prophecies made more sense, and Gilles de Rais had even written a play in 1435 called *The Mystery of the Siege of Orléans*, which glorified Joan as a saint. Unfortunately, after all the dead bodies were found at his home, his plays rather fell out of fashion and it was never performed again.

In 1456, there was a retrial and Joan's visions were declared to be authentic; people who had originally condemned her now vaguely recalled they thought she was holy all along, and the records of the original trial were then burned on the spot. Joan was canonized in 1920, partly as a sop to French pride after they'd just lost about one

and a half million men fighting a futile war in which, this time, for
once, the English were on their side.

After Charles had been crowned king of France, it was decided
that young Henry should have a coronation too, but it was too dangerous to do so at Reims Cathedral, so on December 26, 1431, the
English had the poor child crowned at Notre-Dame in Paris, where
the boy-king rode along streets draped in linen to cover the dirt.
One road was turned into a river of wine filled with mermaids, and
Christmas plays were performed on an outdoor stage.

Inside the cathedral, holy oil was poured from a golden ampulla
(a flask) onto Henry's chest, back, head, shoulders, elbows, and
palms, then dabbed with white cotton, while a white silken cap
was placed on his head, to be worn for eight days (the crown of
St. Edward was thought too heavy for him). Afterward there was a
feast, with guests eating fritters decorated with the fleur-de-lis, symbol of the French monarchy, along with a 'subtlety' showing Henry
being carried by St. Edward and St. Louis, kings of England and
France. At medieval feasts, a subtlety was an inedible dish served
alongside each course that illustrated a theme; the subtlety of the
third course showed Henry being presented to the Virgin Mary and
baby Jesus by saints George and Denis, the third-century bishop of
Paris who became a patron saint of France.

Unfortunately, the coronation was a complete mess. The entire
service was in English and the bishop of Paris had to sit at the back
of his own cathedral, while the banquet turned into a riot as a mob
of half-starved Parisians stormed in to get some free food. The
weather was freezing, the event rushed, was too packed, filled with
pickpockets, and worst of all the food was a disaster, being so old it
was not even suitable to give away to paupers. The *Parisian Journal*, a
contemporary account, lamented: 'The food was shocking . . . most
of it, especially what was meant for the common people, had been
cooked the previous Thursday—the English were in charge . . .
all they cared about was how soon they could get it over and done

with.' The meal was so inedible, even the sick at the Hotel-Dieu complained they had never had such bad food. Well, that's what you get if you have the English in charge.

Then the new king left the next day without pardoning any prisoners or abolishing any taxes, which was the custom at the time.

However, despite the English problems, Charles VIII was not up to much either. 'Physically and mentally, Charles was a weakling, a graceless degenerate. He was stunted and puny, with a blank face in which scared, shifty, sleepy eyes, peering out on either side of a big long nose, failed to animate his harsh, unpleasant features.'[33] He had strange fears, so that on top of his terror of entering a house in case it collapsed on him, he would never cross a wooden bridge (again, wooden bridges at the time probably did collapse quite a lot).

Court life was hardly good for the nerves, either. One of Charles's favorites, Lord de Giac, who also happened to be a poisoner and wife killer, and former love of his mother Queen Isabeau, was dragged naked from his wife's bed and drowned by enemies.[34] Before dying, de Giac asked them to cut off his right hand so that he'd pledged to the devil. Another favorite, Le Camus, was clubbed to death and his hand was also chopped off, which seemed to be a particular French obsession.

In 1431, the English won some small victories and captured a shepherd boy who claimed to be Joan's successor—he had deliberately bloodied his hands and feet in imitation of the stigmata, which rather sounds like cheating. However, the Anglo-Burgundian alliance began to fall apart after Bedford's wife Anne died, and her brother the Duke was insulted that Bedford remarried within months to Jacquetta of Luxembourg. The war was also wrecking England's finances; they were paying huge amounts to Philippe of Burgundy, £150,000 between 1429 and 1431 alone, and they owed another £100,000 to their ally.

Bedford himself died in September 1435, leaving behind a vast collection of books, tapestries, and treasures of various sorts, and was buried in Rouen Cathedral. He was widely mourned in France, with the author of the Bourgeois of Paris writing of him: 'He was always building wherever he went; his nature was quite un-English, for he never wanted to make war on anyone.'

It was all downhill from there for the English. In 1435, the two French factions finally made peace after years of squabbling, and following the treaty between Charles VII and Philippe of Burgundy, all talk of division was banned. In fact, anyone who used the name Burgundian or Armagnac would have his tongue pierced with a red-hot iron. Nothing says national unity more than mutilating anyone who questions it.

The thirteen-year-old Henry VI was sent a letter from the Duke of Burgundy saying the alliance was off, and as he was not addressed as 'king of France' the young monarch burst into tears, which was not the most auspicious sign.

CHAPTER FOUR

To Be a Queen in Bondage

In many ways, the fifteenth century was a fantastic time, likened by one historian to the age of Merrie Olde England; a concept that vaguely alludes to an era when Englishmen and women happily drunk themselves sick under maypoles in twee little villages that resembled Hobbiton before the sour-face Puritans came along and ruined everyone's fun.[35] Certainly it was far better than anything that came before. Real wages had gone up hugely since the previous century and famine would never again hit England. Diseases like leprosy—which affected one in two hundred in the fourteenth century—were being eradicated, and the major cities for the first time had paved roads, as well as drinking water. Hops were imported from Flanders for the first time, whereas previously beer was like a sort of porridge, 'muddy, foggy, fulsome, puddle, stinking.' Playing cards were introduced into Europe from the Middle East in 1379, which is why the kings and queens have the fashion of that era, and the first English laws against playing them were passed in 1497, largely to stop the Wild West-style fights that arose over games.

There was also an education explosion, with a trebling in the number of schools in England in the last century, although they were grim places. Starting at 6. a.m.—in the summer, 5 a.m.—and finishing at 6 p.m., pupils were badly fed, living conditions were spartan, and violence was endemic, although the children could profit from this (a boy in Cambridge was paid 4d to be beaten by a local master as practice).[36] Teachers could be quite rough chaps, and, in 1450, an Oxford schoolmaster went down to St. Michael Church with a gang of schoolchildren to threaten the priest with whom he had a long-running feud. Three years later, the same teacher was arrested for beating up an Oxford local, with the help of two chaplains. Boys at St. Paul's also made money for the school by selling their urine to dyers and tanners.[37]

The middle class was growing in strength, so that in France in the late fourteenth century it was being noticed by observers for the first time that the life of the bourgeois was increasingly better than that of the aristocracy; they did not have the honor and glory of having to fight in wars, but on other hand they didn't have to fight in wars. 'When the vassals must go to join the host, the bourgeois rest in their beds,' the line went.

London's economy was growing, and the city now had a smart shopping street in Cheapside. Thanks to the Merchant Adventurers, so called because they traded abroad, London exchanged goods with countries as far off as Russia, which was then known as 'the land of darkness.' Dominic Mancini, an Italian observer in 1483, wrote: 'London might complain of us for ignoring her as she is so famous throughout the world.' He added: 'there are to be found all manner and minerals, wines, honey, pitch, wax, flax, ropes, thread, grain, fish, and other distasteful goods.'

And while the merchant class was rising, by 1450 England's two thousand aristocrats were going down in the world; ever since the Black Death had wiped out between a half and third of the population, landowning had not been so profitable, and many had to sell bits off to yeoman farmers to make ends meet. These newer men, who became increasingly well-off and able to educate their children, were called 'broggers,' or 'brokers,' and put their money into innovative new homes that were being built. These fifteenth-century houses allowed people privacy for the first time, a novelty where previously little had been done without everyone watching, however disgusting. These new gentry homes had 'a greater profusion and richness of carpets, cushions, tapestries, chests, and beds.'[38]

In a way, the war was the last hurrah for the battle-loving warrior class who had ruled England, and who would soon make way for a new elite of lawyers and tradesmen. As for the poor, towns and villages were filled with beggars, made worse by the increase in enclosures in the 1450s that had left many peasants homeless after their common fields were turned over to sheep farming. Thomas More described them as 'poor, silly, wretched souls, men, women, husbands, wives, fatherless children, widows, woeful mothers with their young babes, and their whole household small in substance and much in numbers.' Corpses were often seen by the roadside, and crime and violence were constant. Mancini wrote of England: 'few venture to go alone in the countryside except in the middle of the day, and fewer still in the towns at night and least of all in London.'

And then came a downturn from 1440 to 1480, which became known as the Great Slump; there was a shortfall in gold and silver because of a lack of bullion and a fall in farm produce, and cloth merchants could not sell their goods abroad. The economic woes were made worse by the king, who was now approaching his third decade and, it was clear, was not like his father.

Nowadays it's supposed that Henry VI suffered from either depression or schizophrenia, but at the time he was just called an imbecile. Henry's illness would later bring on a long period of catatonia, during which he could do nothing, but at all times he was of a nervous and neurotic disposition. Henry was a humanitarian, and would have been better suited to the twenty-first century than the fifteenth; he was disgusted by the sight of a decayed corpse, strictly speaking a quarter of one that had been impaled on a spike, for being 'false to the King's majesty.' Henry thought this cruel, which might be considered fairly normal behavior today, but to everyone at the time it was just thought of as weak. He was 'more timorous than a woman,' in the words of the pope.

When a servant was robbed, he sent him a present of money and asked him not to prosecute the thief, not considered sensible at a time when theft and violent crime were very common. The rudest thing he ever said was 'forsooth, forsooth,' and this after a brutal battle during which people had tried to attack him and killed his closest advisor.

The king was tall and gangling, with a pointed chin and 'mournful, worried eyes, weak in body and mind.' He had no understanding of politics and was under the thumb of Bishop Beaufort. Saintly in many ways and committed to the church, Henry took pity on the poor boys of Berkshire, and at the age of eighteen or nineteen established a school for the underprivileged, which he called Eton. He also founded King's College, Cambridge.

John Blacman, an Eton master who knew him well, wrote of Henry: 'He was, like a second Job, a man simple and upright, altogether fearing the Lord God, and departing from evil. He was a simple man, without any crook or craft or untruth, as is plain to all . . . The King Henry was chaste and pure from the beginning of his days. He eschewed all licentiousness in word or deed while he was young . . . and . . . he kept his marriage vow wholly and sincerely, even in the absences of the lady, which were sometimes very long: never dealing unchastely with any other woman. Neither when they lived together did he use his wife unseemly, but with all honesty and chastity.'

Henry VI even had a fear of nudity. As Blacman recorded, he was once presented with some naked women, an ill-thought attempt by one of his courtiers to organize a male bonding session, which didn't go very well: 'It happened once, that at Christmas time a certain great lord brought before him a dance or show of young ladies with bared bosoms who were to dance in that guise before the king, perhaps to prove him, or to entice his youthful mind. But the king was not blind to it, not unaware of the devilish wile, and spurned the delusion, and very angrily averted his eyes, turned his back upon them, and went out to his chamber, saying "Fy, fy, for shame, forsothe ye be to blame.'"

Henry also hated swearing, insisted on wearing a hair shirt—a mark of holiness—and made each meal start with a chunk of bloody meat in remembrance of Jesus.[39] He wore only black, and went around with round-tied shoes and boots like a farmer's, a long gown with a rolled hood like a townsman's, and a full coat, reaching below his knees. Today that'd be quite a good look if you could pull it off, but late medieval England wasn't quite ready for the Goth/Emo style, and people expected their king to dress in an ostentatious and slightly vulgar way to show off his wealth.[40]

Impoverished and terrified of conflict, the king employed patronage to appease powerful subjects, further undermining his authority and encouraging rivalries; between 1441 and 1449, the monarch created ten barons, five earls, two marquesses, and five dukes. To make ends meet he sold off more and more Crown land, reducing the rents he earned further still.

A medieval society could not function with a weak king, and the people began to fear for their safety from the depredations of rival earls and their entourages, or 'affinities.' This was the era of 'bastard feudalism,' in which lords paid retinues of hired thugs to fight for them, in return for money and protection, without which the population was vulnerable to predators, especially when it came to disputed property. During such conflicts, archers would 'lounge menacingly at the back of courtrooms,' while there was widespread gang warfare over lawsuits and wills.

The Pastons

Much of what we know of the War of the Roses comes from a gentry family called the Pastons, whose letters were discovered in the eighteenth century and are, from a historical point of view, a treasure trove. William Paston was a Norfolk lawyer whose father Clement was born a serf, but his son John became a squire and was connected to some of the feuding aristocrats of the time. Unfortunately, John and his various family members were engaged in a long-running dispute over land with neighbors that often turned violent, and needing the patronage of lords, were drawn into the fighting. John Paston had five sons, the oldest two of whom fought at the Battle of Barnet and had firsthand interaction with many of the leading figures in the war. People at the time were fantastically unoriginal with names, so that over 50 percent of men were called William or John, but John Paston wins some special award, calling his eldest sons John and John, who, for convenience's sake, are known by historians as John (II) and John (III). They decided to go wild with the third one by calling him Edmund.

As well as being financially incompetent, Henry could be incredibly absentminded, too. In 1441, he appointed the Earl of Devon, Thomas Courtenay, as Royal Steward for Cornwall, having forgotten that he had already given the job to a rival called William Bonville. The angry, proud aristocrats of this period didn't really go in for compromise or arbitration, and disputes like these were always likely to end in bloodshed, this one with a private war in Devon and Cornwall between the two lords' men. As the country slid into war, Courtenay became a Lancastrian and Bonville a Yorkist.

Political reasonableness was starting to decline. In 1424, Acts of Attainder had condemned people for treason by simply listing their names in Parliament 'with no evidence produced, no witnessed examined, no defence possible' and these 'became standard instruments of vengeance in the struggle between York and Lancaster.'[41] If an Attainder was approved, the victim was hanged and their heir disinherited; it was described as the legal death of a family, which ceased to exist.

At the same time, things had started going badly in the war. In 1435, the Anglo-Burgundian alliance finally fell apart when Bishop

Beaufort stormed out of a peace congress in Arras leaving the two French groups to negotiate, while the English were drenched in a storm on their way back. The French took Paris in the spring of 1436.

A new dominant figure emerged in the form of William de la Pole, Duke of Suffolk. The de la Poles had started off as Hull wool traders but rose under Edward III, while Suffolk's mother Katherine de Stafford had been related to the Mortimer and Beauchamp families. Born in 1396, Suffolk was a veteran of the war and had been injured at the Siege of Harfleur in 1415 where his father had died of dysentery; later that same year, his elder brother Michael had been killed at Agincourt. In 1429, he had led the English retreat along the Loire, chased by six thousand French soldiers, Joan of Arc, and the Duke of Alençon. Suffolk, after barricading his men inside a fortress and trying to negotiate with Alençon, who claimed not to be able to hear his attempts because of the bombardment of the cannon, was captured. Taken to Orléans, he was imprisoned and ransomed for £20,000, seven times his annual income at least, and only returned to England in 1431.

The Duke of Suffolk—nicknamed Jackanapes—was the largest landowner in East Anglia, and a marriage to Alice Chaucer, widow of the Earl of Salisbury (and granddaughter of the poet Geoffrey), had given him land in Berkshire and Oxfordshire too. He was not a natural leader, but was hardworking and regularly attended the royal council, serving on embassies and in military service in Normandy. From 1433 he was steward of the royal household, which involved running the day-to-day operations of the servants and regular, daily contact with the king. It was a very powerful position, and by 1440, he had the most access of anyone to the monarch. As Margaret Paston said, unless 'ye have my Lord of Suffolk's good lordship, while the werd [world] is as it is, ye can never live in peace without ye have his good lordship.' He rose to become Lord High Admiral in 1447.

Suffolk's main rival was Cardinal Beaufort, whose influence was such that in 1442 he persuaded the council and Parliament to authorize his nephew John Beaufort, Earl of Somerset, to lead an expedition to Maine as Captain General of France and Guyenne. The only problem was that Somerset was not very good, showing a fair degree of incompetence after landing at Cherbourg with seven thousand men and going on an aimless march around France. Most annoying of all, he would not tell his own captains his plans, stating: 'I will reveal my secret to no one. If my shirt knew my secret I would burn it.' Most people thought he probably didn't have any plans. This disaster infuriated the new lieutenant of France, Richard of York, who felt that his authority was undermined. To further anger York, the council told him to have 'patiens and forbere him for a tyme' in regard to the £20,000 he spent of his own money in the war. Soon after his return Somerset died, possibly of suicide, although his feud with York would be inherited by his brother.

Cardinal Beaufort effectively retired, and Suffolk stepped up to the breech, going to France in 1444 and returning with a wife for the king.

Margaret of Anjou

They say opposites attract, and they're wrong. In order to broker peace, Suffolk had Henry wed to Margaret of Anjou, a beautiful and strong-willed French princess who, like pretty much all French queens in English history, was roundly hated. Marrying a domineering French woman to a sex-scared English imbecile was never going to be a fairy-tale romance, and Margaret ended up ruling in his place.

Born in Lorraine, the mixed German-French speaking region that was once called 'Middle Francia' and which the two countries have been fighting over for God knows how long, Margaret was the eldest of ten children to Isabella, Duchess of Lorraine, and 'Good

King' Rene, a jovial womanizer who was, in theory, king of Naples, Sicily, and Jerusalem, as well as Duke of Anjou, although he never actually ruled anywhere. Rene was 'one of the most spectacular royal losers in the fifteenth century,' in the words of one royal historian,[42] and was called 'a man of many crowns but no kingdoms.' In 1431, he set off to win Lorraine and lost, spending three of the next six years in jail and only getting out through ransom. Upon release, he then immediately set off for Naples to claim the throne and spent four fruitless years fighting there before having to leave Italy. His elder brother then died and he became Duke of Anjou and Count of Provence, but he was by this stage utterly broke because of his wars. And so, the future queen had spent most of her early years being looked after by her father's old nurse in the South of France and then near Naples while he was on various escapades, or imprisoned by rival monarchs.

Margaret was fifteen when she was brought over to England in a marriage arranged by Suffolk. In fact, she was married before she even met her husband, with de la Pole standing in for Henry who married her by proxy, since at the time a marriage could take place without one of the parties being present. In front of the king and queen of France, and various French nobility at Tours Cathedral, he took her hand and slipped on the marriage band.

She then set off for England and arrived in Hampshire during a storm, and was greeted by a humble squire who turned out to be Henry in disguise, apparently a family tradition; she was taken to London where there were eight lavish pageants for the queen, with captions in English proclaiming her as the savior of the two kingdoms and a gift from heaven.

On May 30, 1445, Margaret was crowned at Westminster Abbey. The city conduits, built the previous century to bring water for the first time, ran with red and white wine. However, she was too unwell to go through with the wedding ceremony and so Suffolk's wife, Alice Chaucer, had to play the role. So, the couple had two weddings, in which neither of them were both there, and that just about summed up the marriage.

Pope Pius II described Henry as 'utterly devoid of wit or spirit [a man] who left everything in his wife's hands,' and in contrast Margaret was formidable, beautiful, cunning, and ruthless, and feared by the Yorkists more 'than all the princes of the House of Lancaster combined,' according to one chronicler. Raffaelo de Negra, writing to his sovereign the Duchess of Milan, said Margaret 'is a most handsome woman, though' he added, wisely 'she is somewhat dark and not as beautiful as your highness.' Margaret's support for Suffolk and opposition to Gloucester made her unpopular from the start, and on top of this her father had led an army that invaded Normandy, which didn't help her popularity in her new home.

The Truce of Tours, of which the marriage was a key part, was the first peace for many years for the English in France, who according to a contemporary had been 'shut up for years behind town walls or in castles as though condemned to life imprisonment, living in fear and danger.' However, there was a sting in the tail: In July 1445, there was a diplomatic delegation from France, including Rene of Anjou, who demanded that the English keep only Gascony, Calais, and nearby environs. At a second peace delegation in the autumn of that year, the French demanded the English surrender the county of Maine and Henry agreed; Maine and Le Mans were handed over in 1448, which did not seem wise as Maine was peaceful and even loyal and its border was held by a line of strong castles. Suffolk would get the blame for this, even though he opposed it and it was the queen who convinced her husband to hand over the territory.

Humphrey had a great fall

Several leading figures now exited the scene. Bishop Beaufort died in 1447, according to legend offering Death the whole treasury of England in return for more time; Death obviously did not agree, and, considering the state of the country's finances, one cannot blame him. That year Humphrey of Gloucester would suffer a more sordid downfall.

Back in 1441, Eleanor Cobham, Humphrey's wife, had been brought down in spectacular fashion after consulting with astrologers, not an uncommon practice except that one of them had foreseen Henry VI's death. Predicting a monarch's passing was a severe crime that previous kings such as John had executed people for (psychologists today still wrestle with the idea that people tend to predict what they want to hear). Eleanor Cobham was rumored to be conspiring with a priest who was also a 'necromancer'—a dabbler in black magic—as well as one Marjorie Jourdemain, a woman nicknamed the Witch of Eye beside Westminster, to bring about Henry's downfall, using 'devilish incantations and sorcery.' Eleanor was arrested and tried as a witch and heretic, 'and put in perpetual prison,' lucky to escape being put to death as her confederates were; Jourdemain, a 'cunning witch,' who charmed 'feendes and fayries,' was burned at the stake. Cobham was ordered to walk barefoot around the streets of London while carrying a candle for three days in November, forcibly divorced, and sent off to a castle far away. Gloucester was fallen as a result, but worse was to follow.

In February 1447, Suffolk summoned Parliament to his home territory, in Bury St. Edmunds, in exceptionally cold weather. Humphrey came with a retinue of armed Welshmen, but it was a setup; in the words of one contemporary writer, the meeting 'was made only for to slay the noble Duke of Gloucester.' When Humphrey got there, he was prevented from seeing the king and was told to make his way to the abbey infirmary by the city's north gate through a narrow street with the ominous name Dead Lane. He was arrested, along with his more senior servants, on the charges of treason; the country's senior judges were summoned and a trial was hastily concluded.

However, five days later, on February 23, Humphrey was found dead. A stroke seems the most likely cause, although murder can never be ruled out and his body was displayed openly to put off the idea of foul play. A chronicler wrote: 'Some said he died of sorrow; some that he was murdered between two feather beds; and others said that a hot spit was put in his fundament. And so how he died God only knows, from whom nothing is hidden.' Meanwhile several of his household, including his illegitimate son Arthur, were rounded up and convicted of plotting to kill the king and rescue Cobham, but all were pardoned before sentence was carried out. Humphrey's reputation only grew after his death, especially as his enemies made such a mess of everything.

Then in July 1449, Charles VII renewed hostilities and invaded Normandy, partly because of English piracy that Suffolk had encouraged. Rouen fell to the French in October and a sad tide of refugees followed; London filled with families from the continent, some English, some of them French people who had sided with the English and had only known English rule. By April 1450, the English were against the ropes, and at Formigny were slaughtered by a joint French-Breton force. Formigny was the first decisive battle lost by the English since their defeat by the Scots at Bannockburn in 1314, and meant the end of their presence in Normandy after four hundred years of on-off joint rule; the next time British soldiers were seen in Normandy was June 6, 1944.

CHAPTER FIVE

Let's Kill All the Lawyers

At the time of the Normandy disaster, Richard, Duke of York, was in Ireland, sent there largely to keep him out of the way. He was furious, as he was the most important landowner in Normandy and had already spent a fortune on the war, although as he was also the richest landowner in England he was not quite in the poorhouse. Mostly he was angry, though, because he thought the country was being run by incompetents who only got the job through cronyism.

The fall of Normandy now escalated the conflict at home; allied to the Duke of York was his brother-in-law Richard Neville, the Earl of Salisbury, and his son the Earl of Warwick, also Richard Neville. Warwick and Edmund Beaufort, the new Duke of Somerset and the leader of the queen's faction, had an ancient grudge that dated back to when they were married to half sisters and argued over the inheritance.

Salisbury was the son of Ralph de Neville—Westmorland in Shakespeare—an especially brutal man who sired an improbable number of children, at least twenty-two by two wives. His first wife, Margaret Stafford, the daughter of the Duke of Stafford and descendant from the Mortimer clan, gave him eight children before dying in 1396. Just five months later he married again, to the even grander

Joan Beaufort, the daughter of John of Gaunt by his mistress Katherine Swynford, who had in childhood been legitimized and therefore became a powerful landowner. Neville's second marriage produced another fourteen children, including nine sons; however, the two branches became bitterly opposed after he was persuaded by Joan to pass over his sons from the first marriage in his inheritance, and they ended up on different sides at the Battle of Wakefield in 1460.

The Neville family tree illustrates the complex web of alliances of the period. Ralph's sons William, George, and Edward became respectively through marriage the barons of Fauconberg, Latimer, and Bergavenny; this was despite nine-year-old Joan Fauconberg suffering from 'congenital idiocy,' or as she was called at the time, 'a natural fool' (later, in her sixties, a court agreed with a writ that she had been 'an idiot from birth' in the rather unforgiving language of the time). Some of Ralph de Neville's daughters married well, too, to the Duke of Norfolk and earls of Stafford and Northumberland.

But Richard Neville's match was by far the greatest; by marrying the Montacute heiress of Salisbury he became Earl and, on top of this, he inherited from his father the bulk of the family estates, including castles of Middleham, Sheriff Hutton in Yorkshire, and the main Neville home of Raby Castle in Durham, as well as estates in Westmoreland and Essex. Salisbury's eldest son, born in 1428, then became Earl of Warwick through marriage to Anne de Beauchamp, which made him fantastically rich. Warwick held enormous feasts, often feeding five hundred guests at a seating and going through six oxen a day for their evening meal; although it wasn't as sumptuous as one might imagine, as the meat was boiled in great copper vats and salted in case of sieges.

Another of Ralph's children, Cecily, was betrothed to Richard of York at the age of eight and married at thirteen. Cecily Neville was pious even by the standards of the age, attending no fewer than eight church services a day, and bore her husband thirteen children. Although York, whose parents both died when he was very young, could be cold and charmless, they appeared to have a happy marriage.

Across the country there were numerous aristocratic feuds going on, not helped by a weak-minded king who had raised so many people to the peerage, encouraging further the jealousies and intrigues of the court. In the far North, the Percys and Nevilles were rivals. In Devon and Somerset, the Courtenays were rivals with the Beauforts, while further east in the heartland of old Wessex the de la Poles, Staffords, and Mowbrays controlled most of the land, as in East Anglia. The Neville-Percy feud was hugely violent despite various marriages between the two families; likewise, the Nevilles were related to the Somersets, but still fought each other. In 1453, the Courtenay Earl of Devon was also in the middle of a private war against the Nevilles, and had eight hundred horsemen and four thousand foot soldiers at his command.

These baronial conflicts were also fueled by the large numbers of men returning from the war, so many that it was said in the House of Commons in February 1449 that 'murders, manslaughters, robberies, and other thefts, within this . . . realm' are 'dayly [*sic*] increasing and multiplying.' On top of this, England was broke: in the 1440s and 1450s, royal debt continued to mount, up from £164,000 in 1433 to £372,000 in 1449 and £400,000 the following year, at a time when the Crown's annual income was just £5,000 and the royal household cost £24,000 a year.

And just to make matters worse, the queen had still failed to get pregnant, which perhaps is rather unsurprising when Henry did not do anything 'unseemly' toward her.

By the time Parliament met in November 1449, there was huge anger around the country, and York was growing increasingly irate at the court favorites. Public criticism toward the Crown began to be more outspoken, and court rolls record two Sussex farmers, John and William Merfeld, who were brought before a judge for saying 'the king was a natural fool and would often hold a staff in his hands with a bird on the end, playing therwith [*sic*] as a fool, and that another king must be ordained to rule the land.' A reasonably accurate comment, but not the sort of thing medieval governments liked to hear.

Perhaps more worrying was the case of Thomas Kerver of Maidenhead, who was heard to have recruited others to join a plot against the king and was convicted of having 'scheemd [*sic*], imagined, encompassed, wished, and desired and destruction of the king and his realm of England.' Kerver was brought from Reading to the gallows near Maidenhead and was dangling in the noose, waiting to be disemboweled, when word came from the king himself that he should be cut down. Kerver ended up spending a few years in Wallingford Castle before being released.

In 1449, King Henry had been approached by a man called John Harris who was waving a flail—a spiky ball attached to a stick by a chain—beating it on the ground and shouting that the Duke of York should 'fight with traitors at the Leicester Parliament and so thrash them down as he thrashed the clods of earth in that town.' Harris was hanged—such practical advice from the mentally ill was generally not welcomed at the time.

Henry VI's government was dominated by a gang of three: the Duke of Suffolk, Bishop Ayscough, and Adam Moleyns, bishop of Chichester. Within a six-month period all three were murdered by angry mobs.

The wave of violence began in January 1450 when soldiers in Portsmouth rioted and murdered Bishop Moleyns, who was on his way to start a pilgrimage. With his dying words, the bishop rather undiplomatically blamed the loss of Maine on the Duke of Suffolk, as well as all of England's misfortunes. Suffolk was increasingly hated anyway, while in contrast Humphrey had become very popular since his death, and suddenly everyone was retrospectively his supporter; the Abbot of St. Albans expressed the popular opinion when he stated that 'satellites of Satan' had poisoned the king's mind against Gloucester. Suffolk was now blamed for surrendering Anjou and Maine, even though he was against the idea, and it was Henry who insisted on it, genuinely believing in his naive, childlike way that Charles VII wanted peace too.

On January 23, Suffolk spoke at Westminster, denouncing 'the odious and horrible language that runneth through your land' against him. His father had died at Harfleur, he said, his brother at Agincourt, and three more brothers had perished serving the crown; one of them, Alexander, had been killed at Jargeau in 1429, the same year another, John, died a prisoner; a third, Thomas, died in France in 1433 while a hostage. William de la Pole, in fact, was the only one of the five brothers to have survived the war, and he had given thirty-four years of service, during which he had 'continually served about your most noble person.'

But it came to nothing. Four days later, the Commons petitioned the king for Suffolk to be jailed on 'a generalty,' a nonspecific allegation whereby he could be detained without any actual charge being put forward while an impeachment case was put together; impeachment being a charge usually vindictively used to bring down powerful men.

On February 7, Suffolk was formally impeached of 'high, great, heinous, and horrible treasons,' accused of inviting the French to invade, giving away Le Mans and Maine, and having the king release Charles, Duke of Orléans, as well as embezzlement, giving money to the queen of France, and tricking the king into giving him titles and land. All sorts of fictitious stories were thrown about and amassed as evidence; Suffolk denied everything.

He was placed in the Tower of London, but on March 17, King Henry summoned all the lords to his private chambers, where Suffolk protested his innocence and waived his right to a trial in order to plead to the monarch. The king said he did not find Suffolk guilty of treason, only of some lesser charges—misprisions—and so he was only to be banished from England for five years. The Lords most likely supported this, not wanting one of their own to be executed by the Commons. And so, on March 19 he was taken out of the city to his manor in Suffolk, chased by a mob of about two thousand angry Londoners in St. Giles; the rioters, led by a vintner's servant called John Frammesley, shouted that 'the king shall lose his crown.'

Parliament now met in Leicester, and while this happened Suffolk fled the country, setting sail for Calais in the hope of reaching Burgundy, swearing as he left that he was innocent. However, as his boat reached the channel they were intercepted by a royal ship called the *Nicholas of the Tower*, whose sailors took it upon themselves to behead him, although they at least did him the honor of finding a sword befitting his aristocratic status (peasants had to make do with an axe). However, this wasn't much comfort as his executioner, 'one of the lewdest of the ship,' a sailor called Richard Lenard, 'took a rusty sword, and smote off his head within half a dozen strokes.' Two days later his body was dumped on Dover Beach, with the head by it on a pole (as far as anyone knows, this wasn't done as a deliberate reference to his name, although it works).

This was all recalled in a letter sent to John Paston, which was apparently hard to read because it was covered in tears.

Cade rebellion
Then, in May 1450, the county of Kent erupted in rebellion, led by a man called Jack Cade. 'Captain' Cade claimed to be a cousin of the Duke of York, although he was in reality a former soldier and convicted thief from Ireland and something of a liar or fantasist, or both.

There was a rumor that Kent would be held collectively responsible for the death of Suffolk, and that it would be turned into a deer forest as punishment. Extremely unlikely, but the county had also been devastated by the collapse of the wine trade due to the loss of France and the halving of imports, and people were inclined to believe anything. There were also fears of a French invasion, and on April 14 the government had issued a commission of array, which called for a county militia in each hundred (the subdivision of county) in Kent.

The complaints of the Kent rebels were that 'France is lost, the king himself is so placed that he may not pay for his meat and drink, and he owes more than ever any King of England ought, for daily his traitors about him, when anything should come to him by his laws, at once they ask it for him.' By June 6, while Parliament was in Leicester, armed men were assembling around the village of Ashford, and had elected as their captain, Cade, who also went by the names 'Jack Amend-all,' or the aristocratic 'John Mortimer.'

The county of Kent had a relatively large and free peasant class, compared to the rest of England, and they were conscious of their rights and easily agitated, the most recent incident being the 1381 uprising that later became known as the Peasants' Revolt. The Cade rebels were no peasants, however, and among its supporters were seventy-four 'gentlemen,' five hundred yeomen, and lots of merchants and craftsmen; even some MPs supported it. The rebellion must have been large, as some two thousand men received pardons for their part afterwards, so presumably there were many more involved.

Sir William Tresham, former speaker of the House of Commons, was sent to speak to the mob but was ambushed and murdered. Likewise, two groups of lords were dispatched to Kent, one led by Sir Humphrey Stafford, and the other by Viscount Beaumount, constable of England. Sir Humphrey and his brother William arrived with four hundred men but at Tonbridge, on the Kent/Sussex border, the rebels ambushed them and both Stafford brothers were killed. By June 11, the rebels were at Blackheath, on the outskirts of the city; two days later, the leading lords of the country had assembled in London to deal with the crisis, with the king just west of it in Clerkenwell, and negotiations were held with the mob.

However, on June 19 rioting erupted in London and the king—always willing to placate whoever was strongest—allowed for the unpopular James Fiennes, warden of the Cinque Ports and Lord High Treasurer, to be arrested as a traitor and put in the Tower. The Crown also put word around that more arrests would follow, and then on June 25, the council and king simply fled the city, Henry making his way to Warwickshire.

Cade led his men toward London, arriving on July 1 in Southwark and taking over the inns there. Now an uprising had also erupted in neighboring Essex and men from that county had assembled outside Aldgate on London's eastern edge, a repeat of the 1381 revolt when drunken peasants had run amok. Among their demands, the rebels stated that 'it is openly noised that Kent should be destroyed with a royal power, and made a wild forest, for the death of the Duke of Suffolk, of which the commons of Kent were never guilty.' The Cade manifesto blamed the king's advisers for ruining Crown finance, and attacked 'persons of lower nature exalted and made chief of his privy council.' They also had a gripe with purveyance, the forcible requisitioning of goods from ordinary people.

The Kentishmen fought their way across London Bridge against bloody opposition, but once in control of the city, Cade proclaimed that order was to be kept and robbers executed; at Guildhall he set up a court for traitors, with twenty prisoners brought to them, including Fiennes, who was beheaded in the street; Fiennes's son-in-law William Crowmer was then hacked to death, and the heads of the two men were stuck on pikes and made to kiss. Soon Cade was seen riding around London with Fiennes's body attached to his horse.

Meanwhile Bishop Aiscough of Salisbury was murdered by a mob of his own parishioners in Wiltshire on June 29, his crime being to have married the king and Margaret of Anjou, although others accused him of counseling Henry not to 'come nigh her' the queen, which made him responsible for the lack of an heir.

The people of London, frightened of the Kentishmen, rose against the 'multitude of riffraff in the city.' On July 10, Cade was denounced as a traitor, with the vast figure of one thousand marks put on his head, and was tracked down in Sussex by Crowmer's replacement, Alexander Iden, and was mortally wounded near Lewes. The queen, who stayed in Greenwich the whole time, advised the rebels to take offers of pardon, which some did. After it was crushed, the Cade rebellion was punished by the 'Harvest of heads,' with mass executions across the county, Gregory the Chronicler concluding that 'the false traitor the Captain of Kent' was taken and 'upon the morrow he was brought in a cart all naked . . . beheaded and quartered . . . and his head . . . set upon London Bridge.' Afterward, weapons were banned in London and the southeast, although it proved to be unenforceable at a time when men routinely carried knives and there was no police force.

Although the Kentish uprising was spontaneous, the underlying issue was that the people wanted someone else to run the country, preferably someone who wasn't insane. And that person was clearly York, who returned from Ireland in September 1450, marching on Westminster with five thousand men in a show of force. He was popular with the discontented and angry, of which England had an almost limitless supply, and the people behind the Crown already saw him as an enemy. In Wales, York heard rumors that royal servants might attack or arrest him, so he sent the king a bill complaining that he had been treated like a criminal and, despite the king replying with soothing words, he sent another, this one widely circulated in London and reading like a manifesto or one of those pompous open letters people like to send these days.

York was to arrive at the port of Beaumaris in Anglesey, north Wales, where the captain had been ordered to delay him, the Crown convinced he had arrived to cause trouble. Instead he landed in nearby Clwyd and amassed a following there, and he arrived in Stony Stratford, Northamptonshire, on September 23. Richard reached London four days later, and while the Lords and Commons sat, York's men placed badges with his symbol of the falcon and fetterlock (a padlock used for shackling a horse) around town. There was tension in the city between supporters of each side, and after Parliament met again on November 6 there was even a brawl in the chamber, with the Yorkist Lord Cromwell and William Tallboys, a squire of the Duke of Suffolk, exchanging blows.

Edmund Beaufort, the new Duke of Somerset, had now risen to become York's leading rival, replacing Suffolk. The younger brother of the previous duke, Edmund was made a commander in France from 1444, so when York talked about the 'traitors' who lost Normandy, he obviously meant Somerset. After the Cade revolt, Somerset had been put in charge of breaking the resistance in Kent and then was made constable, the highest military post in the county.

On December 1, while having dinner at the Blackfriars house, on what was still then the western edge of the city, Somerset was arrested by Yorkist soldiers and only rescued by the mayor of London, and afterwards placed in protective custody in the Tower. However, York's popularity began to fade, London calmed down, and, in early 1451, Somerset was released.

York, who had the best claim to be Edward III's heir, then used his underling Thomas Young to petition Parliament in May 1451 demanding that he be made next in line to the throne, but the authorities were so angry at the suggestion that Parliament was dissolved and the poor stooge was sent to the Tower for the next nine months.

The Duke of York liked issuing long angry rambling letters, and after the next disaster, the fall of Bordeaux to the French in 1451, he wrote 'Wherefore, worshipful friends, to the intent that every man shall know my purpose, I signify unto you that with the help and support of Almighty God and of our Lady, and of all the company of heaven, I, after long sufferance and delays, it not being my will or intent to displease my sovereign lord, but seeing that the said dyke ever prevailed and ruleth about the king's person and that by this means the land is likely to be destroyed, am fully determined to proceed in all haste against him with the help of my kinsmen and friends.'

York also sent letters to the towns of southern England calling on its people to march to London to remove Somerset. He complained of 'envy, malice, and untruth of the said Duke of Somerset' who 'laboreth continually about the King's highness for my undoing, and to corrupt my blood, and to disinherit me and my heirs, and such persons as be about me.' Etc etc.

The Duke marched to London in February 1452, while Somerset brought the king and his army to meet him, as well as Exeter, Buckingham, and Norfolk, York's former ally. York had demanded that Henry arrest Somerset, and the king agreed, but when he turned up and arrived alone in Henry's tent in Blackheath, he found Somerset still in power; Henry had just gone along with him without really meaning to, because he didn't like confrontation. The royal force was camped at Blackheath, with the Yorkists at Dartford a few miles downstream, armed with cannon and seven ships loaded with baggage. The Duke presented his grievances, mostly against Somerset, who he blamed for the loss of Normandy and for trying to sell Calais to the Duke of Burgundy, as well as charges of embezzlement. Instead York was taken to London as a sort of prisoner, and a rumor spread among his camp that he had been tricked. He was now helpless and vulnerable and by one account was only saved by rumor that his eldest son was marching with ten thousand men from Wales to save him.[43] His eldest son was ten, so even by the violent standards of the time that seems unlikely.

Two weeks later at St. Paul's, York was made to swear a humiliating oath of allegiance to the Crown, announcing that he was a 'humble subject and liegeman' to the king and promising him 'faith and truth as to my sovereign lord' and that 'I shall never hereafter take upon me to gather any routs, or make any assembly of your people, without your commandment or licence.' He was made to lay his hand first on the bible then a cross, just to make sure he wasn't lying.

Parliament was therefore dissolved and York excluded from government, but there were continuing violent disturbances in the neighboring counties. On January 8, 1453, the government attempted to get a grip on the explosion of violence in typical government fashion: by holding a public inquiry, and so putting off any decision.

The fall of English France

In the spring of 1453, the queen finally fell pregnant, seven years after her marriage. Cecily of York wrote to Margaret telling her that her unborn child was 'the most precious, most joyful, and most comfortable earthly treasure that might come unto this land and to the people thereof.' Cecily should know—she had just given birth to her twelfth child and eighth son, Richard; as fate would have it, he would end up bludgeoning Margaret's husband to death. Small world!

Henry, however, now went into a trance, staring into space and totally unresponsive to the outside world, a catatonic episode triggered by the final collapse of the English in the Hundred Years' War, at Castillon, in Gascony, in 1453.

Although during the earlier stages of the conflict the French had relied on cavalry, they had learned from their mistakes and developed better tactics, winning the war not by prancing about on pretty horses, but with discipline and order. This was organized by a man with the appropriately bland name Jean Bureau, or John Office.

They also used guns effectively for the first time. While in the earlier stages of the war guns were used, more often than not they were ineffective and unreliable. Cannons, when fired 'during the siege of Cherbourg it was a matter for congratulations that only four blew up.'[44] Artillery was also in its infancy, with lots of weapons with strange names like serpentines, orgues, crapaudeaux, and rib-audequins. Their projectiles ranged from small pellets to stone balls weighing seven hundred pounds, and some field guns were enormous: Mons Meg, now in Edinburgh Castle, had a caliber of over twenty inches and weighed over fourteen thousand pounds. Guns took a long time to load and ten shots an hour was considered a good rate, but there was a huge breakthrough in the technology around 1370; they could now fire shots at twenty or thirty times the weight of predecessors, and so guns would prove crucial toward the end of the war. A sign of this change came in the 1420s when the heretical followers of Jan Huss fought for Czech independence, becoming the first to use firearms as an effective weapon. Despite the odds, they forced the Catholic forces to sign a peace treaty before inevitably falling to internal divisions between moderates and extremists.

France also developed a standing army, and as a result in 1445, Charles VII at last defeated the free companies, the large groups of English mercenary-cum-hooligans who had been making life a nightmare for everyone for a century. Finally, England's control of Gascony, which dated back to the marriage of Eleanor of Aquitaine and Henry II in 1151, collapsed on July 17, 1453, when John Talbot, the Earl of Shrewsbury, led a surprise attack at Castillon. Talbot, now in his late sixties, was one of the great English commanders of the war; he had been a prisoner of France but been released on *parole*, which literally meant his 'word,' one of the conditions of which was that he could not wear armor against the French—and he kept his word. However, as a result, his head was split open and then a sword was stuck up his anus—and that was basically how the Hundred Years' War ended.

That year arguably marked the end of the medieval period—two months earlier, Constantinople had fallen to the Turks and thousands of refugees had headed to western Europe, bringing with them ancient Greek texts that had been forgotten about in the Latin west.

Castillon also triggered Henry's descent into full madness in August 1453. The king was 'taken and smitten with a frenzy and his wit and reason withdrawn,' and even when the royal baby was presented to him at Windsor, with Somerset as godfather, he showed no signs of recognition. Henry was put under the care of John Arundel, warden of the Hospital of St. Mary of Bethlehem, 'who had studied mental illness and administered a variety of remedies, including laxatives, gargles, potions, poultices, bleedings, and cauterisation to expel "corrupt humours" from his body.' These didn't work, strangely enough.

The country now faced another regency. Meanwhile, on August 24, 1453, the Percy-Neville conflict broke out into open fighting, at a wedding of all places. The spark was the inheritance of Wressle Castle in Yorkshire, which had been built by the Percys in the previous century, but had been confiscated after the Battle of Shrewsbury. On that August day, Sir Thomas Neville, grandson of Ralph and a cousin of Warwick, was to marry Maud Stanhope, whose father held lands that had been confiscated from the Percys by Henry IV, including Wressle. Some one thousand Percy retainers attacked a party of Nevilles on the day of the wedding, although the Nevilles fought them off. The Battle of Heworth Moor, as the wedding became known, was 'the beginning of the sorrows of England,' according to a contemporary, although no one actually died and it was more like a large brawl, the sort found in many small towns after lots of alcohol has been consumed.

CHAPTER SIX

The Fatal Colours of Our Striving Houses

On October 13 Queen Margaret had given birth to a prince, named Edward, after which a great council was summoned; at some point it was decided that York should be invited, and on the 24th a letter was sent signed in the king's name to his 'right trusty and well-beloved cousin.' York was told to put aside his differences with Somerset and to 'come to the said Counsail peaceably and measurably accompanied.'

Inevitably, though, when York arrived at the council he got an ally to launch an attack on Somerset, once again accusing him of treason and demanding his imprisonment. A majority of lords this time agreed, and Somerset was arrested and sent to the Tower; since with the king in a catatonic state he had no protection. Then in January 1454, Margaret pushed herself forward as ruler, publishing 'a bill of five articles' in which she demanded 'to have the whole rule of this land,' the right to make appointments, and an income for her and her son. She also demanded the right to appoint 'the chancellor, the treasurer, the privy seal, and all other officers of this land, with sheriffs and all other officers that the king should make' together with power to 'give all the bishoprics of this land,

and all other benefices belonging to the king's gift.' The queen's bill
was rejected.

Margaret's mother and grandmother had governed Anjou while
her father was held captive on his various failed adventures, and
she had grown up seeing women run things. But although she was
competent, a powerful queen was likely to provoke resentment,
and being foreign (and not just foreign, but French) didn't help. So
instead, on March 27, the Lords agreed to make York protector of
the realm as well as chief councilor, although he insisted on a clause
that stated he didn't want the job, perhaps unique in employment
history. Margaret's son Edward was made Prince of Wales and Earl
of Chester as a concession.

York appointed Salisbury chancellor, but he did try to be
fair in his appointments, and went north to speak to and reason
with the Nevilles and Percys. He also imprisoned his son-in-law
Henry Holland, Duke of Exeter, in Pontefract Castle, for 'a foolish
rebellion' in 1453 against a rival landowner. Holland, yet another
great-grandson of John of Gaunt, was unpopular because of his
cruelty and unpredictability. In a period in which there was some
competition, Exeter was one of the least pleasant figures around,
with a reputation for violence so bad that the torture rack at the
Tower of London, where he was constable, was commonly known
as 'The Duke of Exeter's Daughter.' York also made himself captain of Calais, on top of lieutenant of Ireland. The queen received
lands and offices, as did neutrals such as the Duke of Buckingham
and the Lancastrian Tudors, half brothers of the king. However,
York could not bury the hatchet with Somerset, who was still in
the Tower.

Then on Christmas Day, 1454, Henry left his catatonic state,
and five days later met his son for the first time, holding his hand
and thanking God. He swore he could not remember having the
child, whom he claimed must have been brought by the Holy
Ghost, which made him a laughing stock all over Europe. However,

although he was no longer catatonic, the king was never quite the same again.

On January 26, Henry had Somerset released from prison, with all charges dropped on March 4; York was formally stripped of his role on February 9 and also of his Calais position, which was given to Somerset; Salisbury was forced to resign the chancellorship and Warwick had to release the Duke of Exeter. And so the Yorks and the Nevilles went north to raise an army.

Battle of St. Albans

Somerset arranged for a great council to gather at Leicester, with York and his allies invited, but in mid-May the king's men decided to meet instead at St. Alban's and ordered York, Salisbury, and Warwick to come with no more than 200, 160, and 160 men respectively. The letters reached the three Richards in Royston, just outside of Cambridge, and York replied to Lord Chancellor Thomas Bourchier that 'we intend not with God's grace to proceed to any matter or thing, other than with God's mercy shall be to his pleasure, the honour, prosperity, and wealth of our said sovereign lord, his said land and people' and—York continuing in his rambling way—that having the council at Leicester 'clearly implies a mistrust of certain person . . . therefore, we, his true and humble liegement, have come better companioned, in order to do whatever accords with our duty for the security of his said most noble person, wherein we will spare neither our bodies nor our goodes; and also to know who is suspected of such mistrust, so that we may proceed to the subjugation of those who are guilty of causing such mistrust.'[45] Etc., etc.

The king was surrounded now by a broad group, including neutrals such as the Duke of Buckingham. Outside Ware, a few miles from St. Albans, they heard news that York was nearby with three thousand men, while the king had only two thousand with him. In a last desperate attempt to prevent the country imploding, the king removed Somerset as Constable of England and replaced him with Buckingham. It didn't seem to satisfy York, who from his nearby encampment issued yet more demands.

At 10 a.m. on May 22, Warwick's men began an assault on the town of St. Albans, where the king's banner was raised, signifying that the Crown had declared war on a rebel. It was the first proper battle of the War of the Roses, but the fighting lasted just half an hour; such was the speed with which the Yorkists arrived that the king's men barely had time to get their armor on.

In that short space of time, six thousand men fought with longbows, swords, maces, axes, and poleaxes through narrow streets and even in houses. Most of the battle involved bludgeoning, or the use of battle-axes, to knock men in armor over; once a man was down it was hard to get up, and his enemies would open his visor and put a dagger through his eyes. 'Here you saw a man with his brains dashed out. Here another with his throat cut, the whole street full of corpses,' the abbot of St. Albans, John Whethamstede, wrote, watching events.

During the battle, the fifty-five-year-old Salisbury killed the sixty-two-year-old Henry Percy, the Earl of Northumberland and son of Harry Hotspur; his son Henry, the third earl, would die at Towton six years later, four generations killed successively in battle, losing each time. Edmund Beaufort, the Duke of Somerset, had killed four opponents in hand-to-hand fighting outside an inn when he looked up and felt a sense of doom when he noticed it was called The Castle, recalling that a soothsayer had once warned him about castles; momentarily distracted, he was fatally stabbed. Next to him was his nineteen-year-old son Henry who was wounded and close to death; he survived and would vow to have his revenge on York and Warwick. Percy's cousin Thomas, Lord Clifford, who had been in charge of the barricades, was the other high-profile Lancastrian casualty of the day, and on top of this were 'other divers knights and squires sore hurt.'

One Lancastrian lord, James Butler, the Earl of Wiltshire, reacted in a way many of us would appreciate, taking off his armor and hiding it in a ditch, and then putting on a monk's habit and slinking off. As one contemporary commented, he 'fought mainly with the heels, for he was frightened of losing his beauty'; which having an axe in the head certainly would do.

Henry was put in a tanner's cottage while this fighting played out. The king had spent the duration standing under the royal banner in the market place, a pathetic figure, so much so that even the royal standard bearer had run off. At one point an arrow landed in the king's neck, and he called out: 'Forsothe and forsothe, ye do foully to smite a king anointed so.' For Henry's standards that meant he was really angry.

The king's men began to flee, leaving the monarch sitting on the ground, dazed and wounded. York and Warwick fell on their knees before Henry, calling for a surgeon to help him, and he was respectfully brought down to the local abbey, where survivors on both sides spent the night together, saying a Mass for the sixty dead.

York, having won the debate, was reappointed protector in November 1455 and made Warwick captain of Calais, also giving him some of Somerset's land in Wales. By now Henry was planning his tomb at Westminster Abbey, not a sign of someone hugely optimistic about the future. However, York had to resign on February 25 after failing to secure an act of resumption that would take more land for the crown in order to raise revenue. And he wasn't especially popular. Someone mounted five dog heads in Fleet St. in September 1456, each with a rhyme making fun of York, which rather summed up how many people felt about someone who had brought so much trouble to the kingdom. By the end of the year his allies were replaced in their offices by the queen's.

In August 1456, Margaret and Henry entered Coventry with a display of great pageantry, greeted in verse by men dressed as Alexander the Great, St. John the Baptist, and Edward the Confessor, the eleventh-century king of England who was very holy if rather odd. The man playing St. Edward referred to the young prince as 'my ghostly child, whom I love principally,' while the actor dressed as Alexander greeted the king as 'the noblest prince that is born, whom fortune hath fath,' or favored, which was putting it kindly to say the least. There were also four men dressed as the four cardinal virtues—Righteousness, Temperance, Strength, and Prudence—who pledged their qualities to Margaret. It was now rumored Margaret wanted her husband to abdicate in favor of her son, of whom many 'people spoke strangely,' saying he was a changeling, or maybe a bastard.

Love Day

In early 1458, the king declared that York should suffer for his behavior with a fine of forty-five pounds a year, in order to pay for Masses to be said for the dead. This would be followed by a 'Love Day' on March 25, Lady Day,[46] a well-meaning but rather ineffectual event fashioned by the more moderate men of the council.

Love Day was a typically useless political gesture to iron out impossible difficulties, favored by politicians down the ages. It was hoped to bring together Lancastrians such as Somerset, Northumberland, and Clifford, whose fathers had all been killed at St. Albans, and Yorkists Salisbury and Warwick, who would make reparations to them and agree to keep the peace for ten years. The leaders of each faction walked hand-in-hand to St. Paul's Cathedral; Somerset beside Salisbury, behind them Warwick holding hands with the Duke of Exeter and at the back the king by himself.

They all celebrated a service of thanksgiving at the cathedral, the feeling of love only slightly diminished by the fact that the two sides had turned up with almost four thousand heavily armed men between them; York brought four hundred, Salisbury five hundred, and Warwick six hundred, all wearing red jackets with a ragged staff emblem, while the Percys had fifteen hundred men, Somerset and Exeter together eight hundred. The two groups of soldiers were separated by the walls of the city, while the mayor of London brought a force of five hundred just in case anyone was not feeling the love. Royal archers were placed along the Thames between Hounslow and London, sharpshooters who were ready to fire into the crowd at the first sign of trouble.

It did not make the slightest difference, for the younger Beauforts and Percys carried a 'grudge and wrath' against the Nevilles and York. Later in 1458, Warwick was involved in an accident in Westminster in which a kitchen worker almost stabbed him with a spit, which led to a fight between royal guards and Warwick's men. Warwick claimed it was deliberate and escaped to Calais.

Queen Margaret tried to punish York through an Act of Attainder, which blamed him for all the kingdom's troubles. However, despite the king's revived sanity in 1458, York was not excluded. He still held his Irish position, he received new lands to compensate those that were lost, and his daughter Elizabeth was married to John de la Pole, the fifteen-year-old Duke of Suffolk. Salisbury, meanwhile, was made chief steward of the northern part of the duchy of Lancaster, a vital part of the defense against Scotland. But in the autumn of 1458, the queen removed more Neville supporters from office; Warwick was summoned from Calais in 1459, reluctantly as he feared for his safety, and while he was at court a brawl erupted between the household and his men.

In May 1459, the court went to Coventry again and then across the north and midlands, where Margaret had been building a power base through marriages and appointments, and men loyal to the crown were recruited. The queen handed out her son's livery badge, featuring a swan wearing a crown as a collar, to be worn in battle.

A great council was called in June, but York and the Nevilles refused, and the queen openly denounced them; and so the court in Coventry sent the Hundred Years' War veteran Lord Audley to arrest Salisbury. With this action, the kingdom exploded into violence. York had his wife and younger children evacuated from the North and brought to the relative safety of Ludlow near the Welsh border. Margaret, now in the North raising soldiers, wrote a letter in her seven-year-old son's name to the city of London in which he declared himself 'rightfully and lineally born by descent of the blood royal to inherit the pre-eminence of this realm.' The country was clearly heading for civil war.

CHAPTER SEVEN

Thy Father Slew My Father

Salisbury had recruited an army of five thousand men from his family seat in Middleham in Yorkshire; in the west midlands the Lancastrian Audley raised soldiers from Cheshire, Staffordshire, and Shropshire, between eight and twelve thousand in total, many cavalry armed with helmets, breastplates, and armor. Audley and his troops got to Blore Heath, near Newcastle-under-Lyme in Staffordshire, where Salisbury's troops were dug in across a stream and some hedgerows. The queen had a second army ten miles away led by Lord Stanley, a Lancastrian magnate from the northwest famous for his slipperiness, and his brother William.

On the morning of September 23, 1459, Salisbury began with a feint, and so the queen's men came out only to face a storm of arrows. A second Yorkist charge was repulsed by the Lancastrian bowmen, and at this point the queen's men should have won, having larger overall numbers, but Lord Stanley kept his troops back, wanting to avoid being on the same side as the loser. Lord Audley, despite being in his sixties, got stuck into fighting, and was killed by Sir Roger Kynaston, one of York's men from the Welsh marches whose ancestors had originally been princes of Powys in mid-Wales. He was one of two thousand killed in four hours of fighting, and the site at Blore Heath became known as Deadman's Den, with a stone cross still standing on the spot to this day.

Although a Yorkist victory, Salisbury had lost a lot of men, and his two sons, Thomas and John, were permitted to head back to the family stronghold in the North (only to be captured). Salisbury was also aware that the queen's forces were nearby, and this part of the Midlands was a Lancastrian stronghold, so they could expect little in the way of help. The three Yorkist leaders—Salisbury, Warwick, and York—met at Worcester Cathedral, swearing to protect one another, then went to York's Castle at Ludlow, writing to the king and protesting their 'humble obeisance' and complaining about poor governance, the absence of law, and violence (which, admittedly, took some chutzpah).

Today, Ludlow is a pretty tourist spot filled with tea shops, described by poet Sir John Betjeman as 'probably the loveliest town in England,' and with over five hundred listed buildings (the British equivalent of a National Historic Landmark); but you probably won't get a heart attack from the excitement there. However, in the late medieval period it was something of a happening place, its prosperity built on the wool and cloth trades, and was home to numerous wealthy merchants. Then, on October 12, 1459, two enormous armies turned up, the Yorkists camped by the River Teme, below Ludford Bridge, followed by the Lancastrians, among them Somerset, Humphrey Stafford, Duke of Buckingham and the new Earl of Northumberland, as well as Henry Holland, Duke of Exeter. Despite being married to York's daughter Anne, Exeter was an enemy of the Yorkists throughout the conflict, perhaps because his father-in-law had stuck him in jail. Also encamped with the Lancastrian army were various earls, while the king and queen were in the rear. York's four sons were nearby, his elder two Edward, Earl of March, and Edmund, Earl of Rutland, both of fighting age now, and his younger boys, George and Richard, cared for by his wife.

The Yorkists opened with their cannon, but the battle didn't last very long. In the night, Andrew Trollope, one of Warwick's captains, led his troops across the river to submit. And so before there was even any real fighting, the rebels snuck out of the camp, York and his second son Rutland heading for Ireland, the Nevilles and Edward of March to Calais. The city was the last part of France still in English possession—and would remain so for another century—and as the entry point for trade, and the home of the realm's largest garrison, was extremely important.

Afterwards, Ludlow was sacked, drunken royal troops 'wetshod in wine . . . defouled many women' and the town was 'robbed to the bare walls,' all of this watched by Cecily Neville from the castle; she then had to walk through the streets with her youngest sons George and Richard while the city was still being ransacked, an incredibly dangerous situation for her.

Margaret now tried to destroy York and the Nevilles. She summoned them to a great council at Coventry that she knew they would not attend, which gave her the pretext to attack them. There in November the Queen passed an Act of Attainder during a session known as 'the Parliament of Devils,' which ruined many Yorkists. The Act claimed that Richard of York had been in league with 'Jack Cade, your great traitor' and had come 'out of Ireland with great bobance [arrogance] and inordinate people to your palace of Westminster into your presence, with great multitude of people harnessed and arrayed in manner of war.' It deplored the 'execrable and most detestable deed . . . done at St Albans.'

York was denounced by the assembled members for his 'false and traitorous imaginations, conspiracies, feats, and diligent labours born up with colourable lies.' The Parliament even attempted to claim Henry VI was a great military leader 'so knightly, so manly,' which even his greatest fans must surely have found difficult to say with a straight face—by this stage, Henry could barely do much except drool.

The attainders took away all estates, honors, and dignities from the queen's enemies; among them not just York, Salisbury, and Warwick, but also others such as Lord Clinton, Sir Walter Devereux, and William Oldhall, Countess Alice Salisbury's husband. John de la Pole, Duke of Suffolk, was demoted to Earl just for being York's son-in-law. Lord Stanley, however, was forgiven for some reason. For the winners Owain Tudor—a Welsh knight who had married Henry V's widow Catherine—was given land, and his son Jasper Tudor—the king's half-brother—got the positions of constable, steward, and chief forester of Denbigh, York's former territory in Wales, as well as the right to recruit across the principality. The queen made James, Earl of Wiltshire, cowardly veteran of St. Albans and a staunch Lancastrian, lieutenant of Ireland, but in reality, he had no power there while the Yorkists remained. Henry Beaufort meanwhile was sent to Calais to serve as captain and remove the rebels, but this was easier said than done.

From their Calais base, the Yorkists were able to raid the South Coast and kidnap local officials they didn't like, among them a Lancastrian called Earl Rivers and his son Anthony. In March 1460, Warwick sailed all the way from Calais to Waterford in Ireland to meet York, and on June 26, Warwick, March, and Salisbury landed in Sandwich with an advance party led by Warwick's uncle Baron Fauconberg storming the royal defenses on the 25th.

They once again proclaimed their loyalty to the king—although it was looking a bit improbable now—and repeated the story that Humphrey of Gloucester had been murdered, the conspiracy theory having grown to become fact as time went by. On July 2, Warwick entered London, staying forty-eight hours before his men divided into two large armies, one led by Edward and Warwick, and the other by Fauconberg. Eight days later, Warwick led a Yorkist force to Northampton where they were met by Humphrey Stafford, the Duke of Buckingham, and John Talbot, Earl of Shrewsbury.

After escaping Ludlow, Cecily Neville had taken her sons to her sister Anne, wife of Buckingham, who was not warm to her, their relationship complicated by the family politics of the time. One was married to a Yorkist and one to a Lancastrian, but despite this there were certain rules and Henry VI was merciful, especially to women and children. The Coventry Parliament had confirmed to Cecily an award of one thousand marks a year to comfort 'her and her infants who had not offended against the king.'

The sisters were together when news reached them of the Battle of Northampton and Buckingham's death at the hands of their nephew Warwick. The fight had begun after the king's men took up position in the grounds of Delapre Abbey, just south of the city, defended by a ditch layered with stakes. Warwick sent a delegation to talk. Buckingham responded that 'the Earl of Warwick shall not come to the King's presence and if he comes he shall die'—which ended that negotiation.

The battle began at 2 p.m., with the Yorkists facing both rain and arrows, although the wet weather also meant that the Lancastrian cannons were ineffective. Within half an hour the royalists were all but beaten after one of their leaders, Lord Grey, defected, taking his own men over to the Yorkists and allowing the opposing side to just walk through the Lancastrian left flank; Edmund Grey, yet another great-grandson of John of Gaunt, had been promised the support of the Yorkists in a dispute with the Holland family. Buckingham and Shrewsbury were both killed trying to prevent the king from falling into enemy hands, along with yet another Percy. Some five hundred died—although the common soldiers wearing the livery of Edmund Grey were spared—and poor King Henry was once again discovered sitting in his tent, captured by a lowly archer. Margaret and their son Edward fled to Wales where Henry's half brother Jasper Tudor looked after them.

After the battle was over, one elderly knight and MP, Sir William Lucy, was stabbed to death by a man called John Stafford;

Stafford was in love with Sir William's wife Margaret, who was forty years younger than her husband, although she was also very rich, which must have helped clarify Stafford's feelings. He married her afterwards—she was obviously impressed with his devotion—and Stafford went on to become an MP the following year, the murder having not damaged his political career—although getting killed in battle a few months later did. Margaret became the only woman to have ever been married to two English MPs.[47]

London had now fallen to the Yorkists, with the Lancastrian Lord Scales, a veteran of the Hundred Years' War, holding onto the Tower of London by firing on the city before trying to escape to Westminster Abbey. However, the notoriously unruly London boatmen—the medieval equivalent of taxi drivers—surrounded and murdered him, dragging his naked corpse onto the priory of St. Mary Overie (now Southwark cathedral). York arrived in Westminster on October 10, 1460, with several hundred men, and the Parliament of Devils was overturned; Richard of York now expected to be proclaimed king—yet, when he went to sit on the throne, there were hushes and an awkward silence rather than acclamations.

Even his own followers thought this was a step too far, including Warwick, Salisbury, and the Earl of March, York's eldest son, now seventeen. A compromise was reached in that York would be heir, and Prince Edward disinherited (obviously this didn't take into account what he would think when he grew up). Henry, who now spent most of his days sleeping, agreed, but the queen refused and the war went on. Meanwhile, the Yorkists spread the rumor that the young Prince Edward was illegitimate.

Warwick remained in London, with the king in the Tower, while Edward of March went west to Salisbury (the place) to recruit more men; and York and his second son Edmund, Earl of Rutland, rode to Yorkshire, along with Salisbury (the man). Margaret took her son with her to Scotland in November by ship, where they stayed with Mary of Guelders, the newly widowed wife of James II. In

August that year, Mary had arrived at the siege of Roxburgh Castle, one of the last Scottish fortresses still held by the English, and to celebrate her arrival, the king ordered for his bombards to fire a salute. Unfortunately, one of the guns exploded—as they often did at the time—and the king was fatally hit in the thigh. Afterwards, his wife had the castle destroyed and she now ruled as regent for her eight-year-old son while the Scottish court was feud-ridden, as always.

Margaret learned that her ally Henry, Earl of Northumberland, was raising an army, and sent word to Somerset, Devon, and other loyalists in the South.

Wakefield

York and his second son Edmund spent Christmas in the castle of Sandal, near York (the city) and should have stayed there, but York was tricked into coming out and fighting by the Lancastrian Sir Andrew Trollope, who sent in lots of pretend deserters with messages saying he was going to change sides. In fact, Trollope had five thousand men with him and York was now outnumbered five to one, with John Neville of Raby (descended from Ralph's first wife, and so a Lancastrian), Northumberland, and Somerset facing him ahead, and Exeter on the side, and Clifford closing off the rear. Perhaps he knew it was the end, and after an hour of fighting he sent his son Rutland to flee, and was soon after cut down; his long battle to win the crown had ended in failure and he died just five hundred yards from the castle and safety.

Rutland had gotten as far as Wakefield Bridge when he was stopped by Baron Clifford, whose father had died at St. Albans. Like Rutland, he was a descendant of Ralph de Neville, although through his first wife, but upon discovering his captive's identity, Clifford supposedly shouted: 'By God's blood, thy father slew mine and so shall I slay thee.' Rutland, just seventeen, was killed, appearing as a romantic innocent in a famous Victorian painting.[48]

The Earl of Salisbury tried to bribe his jailers, but 'the common people of the country, which loved him not, took him out of the castle by violence and smote off his head.' Salisbury's son Thomas Neville was also killed, and the heads of York and Rutland were cut off and with Salisbury's were stuck on the gates of the city, York's with a paper crown, along with the sign 'Let York overlook the town of York.'

Edward of March was in the Southwest of England, celebrating Christmas when he was told the devastating news about his father and brother. Tall, blond, and good-looking, Edward was also intelligent and affable; when a Lancastrian force had recently landed accidentally at Calais, Edward had sweet-talked its leader Lord Audley into changing sides, despite Audley's father having been killed by Yorkists at Blore Heath in 1459. And he also lacked the impulsivity that ruined so many aristocrats; rather than heading to Wakefield to avenge his father, Edward stayed put and planned his attack.

March met a Lancastrian force at Mortimer's Cross on February 3, 1461, when 'on the morning there was seen three suns rising' in the sky. It was a parhelion, or sun dog, an optical illusion caused by the sun refracting on ice crystals, and although the soldiers were scared, Edward took it as a good omen, representing the three surviving sons of York and the Holy Trinity. The Yorkists were victorious and March therefore took the symbol of the 'Sun in Splendor' as his personal banner, which became a popular name for pubs.

Afterwards, they captured Henry VI's stepfather, the now elderly Owain Tudor, and took him to Hereford for execution on Edward's orders. The old man was unaware at first what was happening until his captors undid the buttons around his neck, and when he realized the full horror of his fate, he lamented that the head that was to go on a block once lay on a queen's lap. Afterward, his head was mounted on the market cross, where 'an old mad woman got to it, combing his hair and washing off the blood by the light of candles she placed about it, more than a hundred,' which must have added to the general scene of madness in the air (it just happened to be the feast of Candlemass, traditionally the start of spring, so the churches were full of discarded candles).

Although the term 'medieval' has come to signify brutality and inhumanity to modern ears, two centuries earlier, Tudor would certainly have been spared. Chivalry had arisen as a set of rules in the eleventh century as a way of discouraging or at least channeling violence by the aristocratic elite so that, rather than killing their enemies, they ransomed them. For more than two hundred years after William the Conqueror, not a single English nobleman was executed, but that system fell apart in the fourteenth century, while a precedent had been set at Agincourt. Now the cycle of revenge had grown steadily worse, and the rules of war had disappeared, with routine beheadings and the cry of 'kill the nobles, spare the commons.' It is not a coincidence that the most famous book extolling the idea of chivalry, Thomas Malory's *Le Morte d'Arthur*, was published during the War of the Roses, because like many concepts it only became celebrated as it was dying. Malory had been a soldier in Gascony and served as an MP for Warwickshire, but after a feud with the Duke of Buckingham, he was indicted for cattle rustling and 'deer parching.' He also spent time in Newgate jail, according to one account, for 'extortion, rape, cattle rustling, and robbery,' suggesting he had slightly fallen below the standards of chivalry. Finally, in 1468, Malory was in trouble for conspiring against the king, and was sent to jail where he wrote his famous work about King Arthur.

Queen Margaret had now raised soldiers in Scotland, having agreed to hand over Berwick in exchange for an army, perhaps not appreciating what a terrible prospect this was to the people of England, who feared the men north of the border, and with good reason. On top of this, because she was short of funds to pay them, she had agreed that anyone who signed up could freely plunder once they had crossed the River Trent, which marked the southern extent of the north of England. The southern English also feared the people beyond this river and John Wheathampstead, abbot of St. Albans in Hertfordshire, spoke in horrified terms of 'Northern people, faithless people, people prompt to rob.' He described the 'northern invasion' as being worse than Attila's Huns, the terrifying barbarians from the late Roman period. The prior of Croyland in Lincolnshire feared 'an execrable and abominable army' coming down from the north 'like so many locusts.' To make things worse, the winter of 1460–1 was especially harsh, and Margaret's Scottish army was hungry; by January 12, it was already pillaging villages and the queen did not stop them as some of the land belonged to York anyway. Soon rumors spread south of a monstrous army of northern savages.[49]

Warwick, meanwhile, raised money in London and the Southeast by asking for help against the 'misruled and outrageous people in the north parts' who were 'coming toward these parts to the destruction thereof.' The Yorkists did have some support in the northern counties, and the Lancastrians in the South, but most of their soldiers came from different ends of the country, and this helps explain the savagery of the fighting. When, in late 1460, the royal army headed south from Wakefield, there was a genuine terror in the capital that they would sack the city. Songs of the period recall the threats of northern men violating southern women, and of 'the lords of the North' coming to 'destroy the south country.' In preparation for this barbarian army, the Earl of Warwick's troops had prepared wildfire, mantraps, nets, caltraps (steel starfish), and guns that fired arrows, although as it turned out all these gadgets 'would prove useless'—Warwick loved using the latest weaponry, but there were always problems with it.[50]

Warwick now led an eight thousand-strong army out of London, along with his brother John Neville and uncle Fauconberg; as well as the Duke of Norfolk, he had John de la Pole, Suffolk's son and

York's son-in-law through marriage to his daughter Elizabeth, and Warwick's brother-in-law Arundel. He also had the king as prisoner.

The two sides met on February 17, 1461, at the second Battle of St. Albans, and although Warwick's Burgundian soldiers were armed with hackbuts, which fired lead shots—the first use of hand-guns in England—the slightly larger Lancastrian army won. The fighting went on until 6 p.m., by which time darkness had made it impossible to fight and Warwick and the Yorkists fled. King Henry spent the battle laughing and singing to himself, a huge military asset as always.

Afterwards, the king's former captors Lord Bonville and Sir Thomas Kyriell were brought before the queen and her seven-year-old son Prince Edward. He was asked: 'Fair son, by what manner of means shall these knights die?'

'Let their heads be taken off,' the little monster replied, and got his wish—the two men were beheaded in front of them. Bonville and Kyriell had been ordered to guard the king by Warwick, but had not behaved dishonorably and had treated him well. Bonville replied to the boy: 'May God destroy those who taught thee this manner of speech.'

Thirty-one men were knighted after the battle, including the young prince and Andrew Trollope, the man who had changed sides back in Ludford, and boasted to the queen in the humble-brag of the day: 'My Lord, I have not deserved it, for I slew but fifteen men, for I stood still in one place, and they came unto me.'

On the same day, the Speaker of the House of Commons Thomas Thorpe was lynched by a Yorkist mob and beheaded in Harringay Park, five miles north of London.[51]

Queen Margaret descended on London, just ten miles away, with Edward of March in the Cotswolds, but she then made a mistake by stopping outside for fear of what her Scots army might do in London, the men having already ransacked nearby Westminster and Southwark. She could not give enough reassurance to

Londoners, only vague promises that 'the king and queen had no mind to pillage the chief city . . . but at the same time they did not mean that they would not punish the evildoers.' Even when the city council organized a food convoy to be sent to the royal army, an angry crowd stopped it, while there were rumors the Yorkists were on their way. And so Margaret now pulled her army back by twenty miles and withdrew north—and on February 26, the Earl of March simply rode in from the west and was proclaimed King Edward IV.

George Neville, bishop of Exeter, spoke in St. John's Fields, just outside of the city, and asked the crowd if they wanted Henry to remain as king. 'Nay! Nay!' they shouted. When asked if they wanted Edward of March, they shouted back: 'Ye! Ye!' And so, on March 3 at Baynard's Castle, a small number of lords and bishops agreed to his claim, and the following day at St. Paul's the *Te Deum* was sang. Edward was aged just eighteen.

Towton

Edward now brought an enormous army, of up to forty-eight thousand men, to Towton in Yorkshire, facing at least forty thousand of the queen's soldiers (figures vary—the Lancastrians may have had as many as sixty thousand, although then, as now, people always exaggerate numbers). Afterward, some sixty knights and gentlemen were attained and of these, twenty-five were MPs, which suggests that there probably were a lot of people at the battle.

Once again, the fate of the kingdom depended on the unpredictable English weather, this time a snowstorm.[52] The day before the main battle on Sunday, there was a warm-up when the Lancastrians attacked Yorkists who were rebuilding a bridge on the River Aire. Edward ordered more men to reinforce the bridge while sending a group led by Fauconberg three miles upstream to cross and chase the Lancastrian Lord Clifford. Clifford went to drink a glass of wine, taking off his neck guard, and was killed instantly by a sniper.

The following day, Palm Sunday, Edward took up the standard and in a blizzard[53] won the most violent battle in English history. It began at 10 a.m. when Fauconberg ordered archers to shoot one arrow each and then withdraw out of bow shot. When the Lancastrians fired back, they found the wind blowing against them and their missiles 'came not near the southern men by forty tailor's yards.' Fauconberg marched his archers forward, taking some spent arrows to use and leaving others in the ground to hinder any attack.

Then the main fighting began, and the Lancastrians were forced against the River Cock in what became known as Bloody Meadow: aptly so, as by the end of the day there were up to twenty-eight thousand dead, among them Andrew Trollope, leader of the Lancastrian forces. The Earl of Wiltshire, who had run away from St. Albans and then Mortimer's Cross, fled from Towton, but was captured at Newcastle and beheaded.

Before the battle, the Lancastrians had knocked down the bridge by Cock Beck, on the river Cock (sadly since renamed the River Wharfe) and now they were trapped; many jumped in the frozen river, where their heavy armor ensured their deaths, and it was only when the river dammed because of the number of corpses that anyone could escape. Afterward, it became known as the Bridge of Bodies, adding to a whole lexicon of poetic names the war had inspired.

Bishop Neville thought the death toll to be twenty-eight thousand, far higher than the most famous of English battles, Hastings, which saw about six thousand fatalities, but it was probably nearer to twenty thousand. At any rate, there was 'an area of bloodstained snow six miles long and [an area] three miles wide was covered in corpses.' The battle was followed by numerous executions, forensic evidence has suggested, with at least two dozen knights and countless more men put to death. Some of the skulls found at the scene were split in half, or had multiple holes; many were mutilated after the battle. It was said afterwards that a trail of blood marked the twenty-three-mile road from Towton to York.

The new king then marched on York where he was greeted with the heads of his father and brother; they were now buried, and in their place were put the heads of Devon and Wiltshire, that month's out-of-favor aristocrats.

A sad trail of Lancastrians headed toward Scotland, and close to Bamburgh Castle Queen Margaret and her son were separated from the rest of the group. According to one (admittedly highly dubious) story, a gang of robbers attacked them and were ready to cut her throat when Margaret fell to her knees and pleaded: 'I am the daughter and wife of a king, and was in past time recognized by yourselves as your queen. Wherefore if you now stain your hands with my blood, your cruelty will be held in abhorrence by all men in all ages.'

It turned out that Black Jack, as the man was called, was a former Lancastrian soldier, and it was now his turn to get on his knees and swear to take her to safety, which he did, to the Scottish border at Kirkcudbright. There, Margaret would remain for the time being, so poor that she had to borrow a groat from an archer to make an offering on her saint's day.

CHAPTER EIGHT

This Sun of York

That the Yorkists won was down to the support of London, which was vastly richer than anywhere else in England, due to its role in the export of wool and other staples. In the nine months before Towton, the city provided thirteen thousand pounds for the Yorkist cause, enough to pay twenty-six archers for twenty days' service.[54]

And now the city merchants had a king worthy of the name, the very opposite of the dull-witted Henry in every respect. Edward of March, also known as Edward of Rouen after his birthplace, had been born in Normandy but raised mostly in Ludlow. He had inherited his mother's good looks and was 'very tall . . . exceeding the stature of almost all others, of comely visage, pleasant in expression, broad chested.' As well as being a giant—he stood at six feet, three inches—Edward was handsome, fair-haired, and blessed with charisma and natural affability, as well as a winning smile. He 'was so genial in his greeting, that if he saw a newcomer bewildered at his appearance and royal magnificence, he would give him courage to speak by laying a kindly hand upon his shoulder.'[55] He also had that knack of remembering the names of everyone under him, as well as something about them with which to make small talk.

Knowing how powerful the city of London had become, the new king took leading merchants away for team-bonding weekends, where they played sports in the morning and drank themselves senseless in the afternoon. These male-bonding sessions would involve risqué jokes, but also had a more sordid side, with women passed among them—for in sexual matters Edward was also the opposite of his predecessors, a compulsive womanizer with a string of illegitimate children.

Italian chronicler Dominic Mancini heard that Edward seduced women with money and promises, 'pursued indiscriminately married and unmarried, noble and low-born,' and supposedly tricked one highborn woman, Lady Eleanor Butler, into his bed by promising her marriage; this would cause problems later. Another Italian, Polydore Vergil, said Edward tried to rape one of Warwick's relatives under his roof, although Mancini said he never used force, only lies, and then 'as soon as he grew tired with the affair,' he passed them onto other courtiers. According to French diplomat Philippe de Commynes, the king of England 'thought nothing but upon women, and that more than reason would, and on hunting, and on the comfort of the person.'

Edward boasted he had three concubines, each with a special gift, 'one the merriest, another the wisest, the third the holiest harlot in the realm, as one whom no man could get out of the church lightly to any place but it were his bed,' according to Thomas More, writing in the reign of Edward's grandson, the equally corpulent and sex-mad Henry VIII. The king's favorite was Jane Shore, who was famously promiscuous and kindhearted.

In contrast to Henry's dreary and pious court, Edward's was like a teenage boy's vision of being in a music video. Sitting on the marble throne, he was attended by four hundred men under the control of the Lord Chamberlain, while the Knights of the Body looked after his personal needs. Each day, he would sit in the King's Chamber, where in the morning two thousand people ate at the king's expense with servants on hand with water and thirteen minstrels playing quaint medieval music; Edward was a big fan of minstrels and even established a guild of minstrels after his own minstrel livery, the forerunner of a brand label, was usurped by 'certain rude husbandmen and artificers.' Edward also loved gold and had a toothpick made of it, and having it garnished with diamond, pearls, and rubies because it was believed the gemstones could be used to detect poison as they became moist with contact.

This was an era of outlandish fashions, with pointy shoes, ostentatious and vulgar rings, and enormous belt buckles, which young men thought made them look dangerous and sexy (The long pointed shoes of this era only became fashionable because one count of Anjou had them made because he had bunions, according to one theory.) The king himself was a great lover of fashion and in the first year of his reign had his keeper of the great wardrobe spend £4,784 on clothes and furs for the king's person, at a time when the average annual wage of a laborer was six pounds. He even employed a man to jump on his bed after he had woken up to ensure it was wrinkle-free.

The king was a dashing young warrior, but he would eventually become disgustingly overweight, booze-addled, and worn out by relentless womanizing. The Crowland chronicler, an unknown monk living in the midlands, 'marvelled that such a gross man so addicted to conviviality, vanity, drunkenness, extravagance, and passion could have such a wide memory that the names and circumstances of almost all men, scattered across the kingdom, were known to him, just as if they were daily within his sight.' But while the new king could be jovial and even cultured—he admired and supported the arts—he also had a dark and violent side.

A new regime meant the spoils for the victors. Edward's cousin Warwick, known to history as the 'kingmaker' because of his role in establishing the Yorkist regime, became the richest man beside the monarch. Edward's uncle Fauconberg became Earl of Kent and Warwick's brother John Neville was made Lord Montague and Earl of Northumberland, a former Percy title. Another brother, George Neville, was promoted to archbishop of York, the second highest position in the English church, celebrating with a feast in which six thousand guests ate for days, with one hundred oxen washed down with twenty-five thousand gallons of wine (about 150,000 bottles).

Edward's closest friend William Hastings, who had fought alongside him at Mortimer's Cross, was made chamberlain of the household and 'gatekeeper to the king's presence.' He was also given the title 'Lord Hastings of Hastings' as well as Hastings Castle in Sussex, even though he had no actual connection with the place; nominative determinism, you might say. Hastings was described by Thomas More as an honorable and chivalrous man, but with a depraved private life. He was in charge of 'organizing the royal amusements,' which was something of a euphemism, and was considered a bad influence by Edward's wife, for he and the king shared 'compulsive tastes for wenching.' Now ennobled, Hastings chose as his emblem the symbol of a man-tiger, a creature with the body of the big cat but with Hastings's face—along with a comically giant penis.

Edward's youngest brother Richard was made a Knight of the Bath, which literally involved him getting in a bath, as well as having his hair cut by a barber who 'took the bath as his fee' after Richard had been in it. After this, the young royal spent the night at church and was then presented to the king whereupon two knights fastened his spurs to his heels.[56]

As for the losers, some Lancastrians were still in exile, including the Duke of Exeter and Chief Justice Sir John Fortescue, the former now reduced to begging in Bruges. Others, such as Henry Stafford, the second son of the Duke of Buckingham, were pardoned; but some twelve peers and one hundred knights and squires were declared outlaws.

Leading Lancastrian Henry Beaufort, the new Duke of Somerset, was captured in 1462, but Edward treated him well.

Fifteenth-century London mayor William Gregory wrote that Somerset 'lodged with the king in his own bed many nights, and sometimes rode a-hunting behind the king, the king having about him not passing six horse[men] at the most and yet three were the duke's men.'[57] There is nothing sexual implied by this, as people would often share beds as they were expensive and so precious. In fact, there was so little furniture at the time, even among royalty, that Richard III even took his bed on campaign with him, his money chest stored inside in a secret compartment. The word 'chairman' reflects the fact that furniture was rare enough that only the most senior person could use it.

Six months after Somerset's capture, his lands were all returned, and some Yorkists were unhappy at how they were not rewarded and their enemies not punished. Somerset and Edward did have womanizing in common, but it wasn't enough of a bond, for as Gregory wrote: 'The king loved him well, but the Duke thought treason under fair cheer and words.' It all went wrong when Edward took his new friend with him to Yorkshire in 1463, but along the way in Northampton, which the Lancastrian army had sacked in 1460, some locals tried to lynch 'the false Duke and traitor,' as they called him. Edward pacified the mob with a casket of wine while he snuck the Earl out of the city. After this, Somerset went back to the Lancastrians, fleeing to Wales in search of other rebels

Plots continued against the new monarch. John de Vere, the Earl of Oxford, was arrested in February 1462, along with his eldest son Aubrey, for conspiracy to overthrow Edward with the help of the French, after letters between Sir Aubrey and Queen Margaret were found. Father and son were drawn on a hurdle from Westminster to Tower Hill, and hanged on a scaffold eight feet high to give the crowd a better view. Strangely, Edward then tried to woo Aubrey de Vere's brother John, rather hoping that despite all these past disagreements he might become a loyal follower. And so, in 1465 at the coronation of the new queen, Lord Oxford officiated as

Lord Great Chamberlain of England, which had been an ancient privilege of the de Vere family for centuries.

Meanwhile, Queen Margaret continued to keep the Lancastrian cause alive, although it looked increasingly pathetic. To start with, they had the sympathy of the new French king, the wily and devious Louis XI, who had come to the throne after his neurotic father Charles VII died in 1461 after starving himself to death for fear of poisoning. Louis, known as 'the universal spider' because of his devious manipulative character and network of spies, was a model for Machiavelli's book *The Prince*.

While in Scotland, Margaret had at first sent Somerset as her messenger to the French, but when he arrived in Paris he rather unwisely boasted that he had slept with the queen of Scotland, Mary of Guelders. King Louis, a relentless schemer, sent him back to Margaret without any promises, and helped to spread stories of his boasts until they reached Queen Mary; she was so angry at Somerset's absurd allegations that she had a lover that she tried to persuade her actual lover to murder him.

Edward took the threats seriously, and in a March 1462 letter to London aldermen warned that 'the people, the name, the tongue, and the blood English' would we wiped out by his 'adversary Henry,' moved 'by the malicious and subtle suggestion and enticing of the said malicious woman Margaret, his wife.' He warned she was going to lead a huge army with thousands of foreign soldiers from Spain, France, Scotland, Portugal, Denmark, and Italy who would invade England and presumably commit unspeakable acts. In fact, in October that year she did invade Northumberland but with just a few hundred men and had to flee again.

The reason was that Louis had lost interest in helping Margaret; their deal had featured a secret clause to hand over Calais to France, but without the cooperation of the Duke of Burgundy, whose land surrounded the port, this could come to nothing—so Louis gave up to concentrate on other plots. By the winter of 1463, Margaret was reduced to a pathetic band of followers based 150 miles east of Paris in the middle of nowhere, desperately going around trying to get support and money. They were so amateurish that an attempt to get help from the Portuguese went wrong because no one could remember the name of the king of Portugal.

And so Henry, Duke of Somerset, rode to Northumberland to meet Henry VI to start a new revolt at Hedgeley Moor on April 25, 1464, a battle which ended in disaster for the Lancastrians. Ralph Percy, a grandson of Hotspur, was killed by a force led by John Neville, third son of Salisbury, muttering the rather ambiguous last words 'I have saved the bird in my bosom.' Ralph was one of four sons to the third Earl killed in battle between 1460 and 1464, three in battle; Henry and Richard Percy were killed at Towton and another, Thomas, at Northampton.

Soon afterwards, at Hexham on May 15, John Neville led a force of three to four thousand men against a much larger Lancastrian army, many of whom drowned attempting to escape over a stretch of river called the Devil's Water. Somerset was captured and beheaded, his title passing to his brother Edmund; he left a bastard son, who became the ancestor of the dukes of Beaufort, but with him dead, the Lancastrian cause was too.

In August 1464, the Percy family stronghold, Alnwick Castle, one of three fortresses still in Lancastrian hands after Towton, surrendered to Warwick; another castle, Dunstanburgh, had tried to hold out, but its defenders were soon taught an important lesson about how the new cannons made such fortresses outdated. Today it's a ruin.

Afterward, Henry VI was smuggled back into England, hiding in Bamburgh Castle. He then traveled to another fortress, Bywell, before staying in a Cumbrian manor and then with some monks. Eventually King Henry was caught at Waddington Hall in Lancashire, but managed to escape with some servants before being captured again on July 13, 1465, by the River Ribble at the wonderfully named Bungerly Hippingstones. The deposed king spent the next five years as a prisoner in the Tower of London, where he was given five marks a week pocket money, as well as wine. He seemed relatively happy.

The last place to hold out, however, was Harlech Castle in Wales, which repulsed the Yorkists until Lord Herbert finally captured it in 1468, the captain being taken to London and beheaded, along with others. It was the longest siege in British history, and inspired the song 'Men of Harlech' (most famous for being sung by Welsh soldiers in the film *Zulu*).

However, there was trouble brewing at the Yorkist court. Prospero di Camulio, a Milanese visitor, said that anyone who reflected upon 'the victors' state of mind' should 'pray to God for the dead, and not less for the living.' He predicted 'grievances and recriminations will break out between King Edward and Warwick' and 'King Henry and the Queen will be victorious.'

The cause was love.

Hasty marriage seldom proveth well

In the spring of 1464, soon after the defeat of Somerset, King Edward was riding north to meet Scottish ambassadors when he stopped off in Buckingham and disappeared to go 'hunting.' In fact, he had gotten married in secret instead.

After the bloodshed, Edward had pardoned many Lancastrian lords, including one called Lord Rivers, who was given his lands back within a year, as was his eldest son Anthony, both even being allowed to join the king's council. The family had fought with the former king, while Rivers's daughter Elizabeth Woodville had lost her husband Sir John Gray in the fighting, leaving her impoverished—and one day Elizabeth took it upon herself to ambush the new king while he was out hunting to get her husband's lands back.

Elizabeth Woodville was a beautiful schemer with long blonde hair and blue eyes, which were 'heavy-lidded like those of a dragon;'[58]

as was common at the time, she shaved her hairline to make her fore-head look bigger, which was considered more attractive. The king was enraptured, and by some romantic accounts tried to take her by force, only for her to stick a knife to her own throat[59]—fifteenth-century ideas of romance being somewhat different to modern ones, clearly. He backed down, and when his attempts to make her his mistress failed, he did the unthinkable, by marrying her in secret.

It was a remarkably idiotic move, and when Edward told the council that he was married there was at first laughter; no king had wed a commoner for four hundred years. That's what Elizabeth's father Earl Rivers, or Richard Woodville, had been born. (She was also the first English-born queen since 1066.)[60]

Then there was outrage. Marriage was for the purpose of alli-ances, not for love (or lust). Woodville was Lancastrian, already married and with two kids. Although Jacquetta of Luxembourg, Elizabeth's mother, came from continental aristocracy—she had previously been married to the Duke of Bedford—her father, Lord Rivers 'was generally regarded as an arrogant arriviste and blood-sucking parasite who lived shamelessly off his wife's dowry.'[61]

In particular, this infuriated Warwick, who was in the process of negotiating a marriage with a French princess when he heard the news. Edward's cousin was fourteen years older than the king and so influential that in 1464 a senior courtier told his mas-ter Louis XI in that characteristically crushing way the French like: 'they tell me they have two rulers in England—Monsieur de Warwick and another, whose name I have forgotten.' Warwick owned over one hundred manors in twenty-one counties and was also captain of Calais, warden of the Cinque Ports, warden of the Eastern Marches, and admiral of England. He was 'arrogant even by fifteenth-century standards' but also had the common touch and was popular, especially on the South Coast where he had gotten rid of pirates; that's partly because he was a sort of pirate himself.

That the king did not inform his cousin before making such a decision was obviously insulting, and many believed that Woodville must have used some sort of witchcraft. The night before the May 1 wedding of Edward and Elizabeth was one of four Sabbaths in the witches' year—the Germans called it *Walpurgisnacht*—and sorcerers apparently met under oak trees, as Edward and Elizabeth had first done, so it all sort of made sense. People felt that she had bewitched him, although the more obvious explanation is that Edward was a young male who was thinking with his heart, or another organ important to men his age.

Warwick had wanted him to marry Mary of Guelders, dowager queen of Scotland. Unfortunately, she was too old and too immoral, and by the time the plan was formulated, too dead. Edward also turned down the opportunity to marry twelve-year-old Lady Isabella of Castile; she instead went on to wed Ferdinand of Aragon, so uniting Spain. Isabella never forgave this apparently, and twenty years later her ambassador told the English representative that she 'had turned her heart from England' as a result. Philippe the Good, Duke of Burgundy, had also suggested to Edward a marriage to his niece, a daughter of the Duke of Bourbon who was apparently beautiful.

So, when the king announced the big news, Warwick had come expecting to be asked to go to St. Omer to meet Louis XI for the marriage conference; Warwick's aim was to thwart Margaret of Anjou's attempts to have her own son Edward betrothed to a French princess, and the king's marriage was his prime diplomatic bargaining tool. Instead he'd just thrown it away.

Rivers and Warwick were also old enemies, dating from the time when the former had been in charge of the Calais garrison and refused further orders until they had been paid. At Calais, Warwick and Edward had also held Lord Rivers as a captive and mocked him, calling him 'knave's son.' Cecily Neville also strongly objected to her son's marriage, and with good reason, for the Woodvilles were seen as overmighty and unpopular. Elizabeth was, in the words of one historian, 'calculating, ambitious, devious, greedy, ruthless, and arrogant.'[62] She was so haughty she dined publicly in silence and during her three-hour meals all the ladies-in-waiting had to stay kneeling, including her mother and the king's sister Margaret, although those two could at least rise after the first course. This in particular infuriated Edward's two brothers.

The royal couple went on to have a happy or at least productive marriage, with ten children, although the womanizing continued, and he had at least five illegitimate offspring. Elizabeth, understandably, was hostile to a number of Edward's cronies, in particular William Hastings, who she considered a bad influence on her husband. As Thomas More said, 'women commonly not of malice but of nature, hate such as their husbands love'—especially when their husbands love to go 'wenching' with them.

In September 1464, Elizabeth was proclaimed queen and she was crowned the following May. Among those at the coronation were the new consort's youngest sister, seven-year-old Catherine, and her ten-year-old fiancé Henry Stafford, heir to one of the leading dukedoms of Buckingham. The Woodvilles had won the right to marry Stafford to one of their numerous daughters.

Also that month, Elizabeth's sister Margaret was married to the heir of the Earl of Arundel. By 1467, five more Woodville sisters had married peers, among them Mary to the Herbert family heir, which meant the Herberts could rely on Woodville support in their ongoing feuds with Warwick in south Wales. The Earl of Warwick was also jealous of the Woodvilles because his two daughters had trouble getting matches due to so many men marrying Woodville girls. Elizabeth had eleven living siblings in total, whom Edward felt obliged to help marry off: the most outrageous came in January 1465 when John Woodville, her twenty-year-old brother, was paired with the sixty-six-year-old Catherine Neville, the king's aunt, a match known as 'the diabolical marriage.' Neville, 'a slip of a girl almost four score years old,' as a contemporary noted with some sarcasm, already had three dead husbands and several children older than their new step-father, and even her grandson the Duke of Norfolk was a year older. She had been widowed at thirty and her second husband, Thomas Strangeways, had been the servant of her first.

They weren't entirely a bad lot. Anthony Woodville, Elizabeth's eldest brother, was a renaissance man who translated books into English. Anthony Woodville, also called Lord Scales, had a long military record, having fought against the Saracens in Portugal, had also been on pilgrimage to Santiago de Compostela and Rome, and was on good terms with the pope.

Scales was also a champion jouster, and took part in the biggest sporting event of Edward's reign in June 1467 when the king arranged for him to fight the greatest swordsman in Christendom, Anthony, 'the Grand Bastard of Burgundy' (he was the illegitimate son of the Duke but the nickname was not an insult). Edward had purposely tried to bring jousting back to entertain the masses, the sport having rather gone out of fashion from its hugely violent heyday in the thirteenth century. Gravel and sand from the banks of the Thames was carted to Smithfield and a viewing platform built by carpenters; the Grand Bastard was given rides along the river in a barge with gold cloth, and slept in a gold-draped bed.

Before the event, Scales was coached by a famous old knight, Sir John Astley, who, in 1438, while jousting a rival, Pierre de Massy, had accidentally driven his sword through his head. (He wasn't punished, although he had also spent four years in jail for another matter.) On day one, the Grand Bastard's horse died after it rammed its head against Scales's saddle, pinning the visitor to the ground, and afterward Scales had to prove he used no illegal equipment after there was suspicion. Scales and the Grand Bastard then discarded some armor and attacked each other with swords, after which they retired for the evening. The next day they fought with spears, then axes, but 'the King beholding the casting spears right jeopardous and right perilous, said, in as much as it was but an act of pleasaunce, he would not have none such mischievous weapons used before him.'[63] At one point, the king cried in a high voice 'whoo!' such was the excitement, and after the fighting with battle-axes had become so violent he had to intervene before one of them was killed; he also refused their request to fight on with daggers. It ended with their embraces, a save of face that left everyone happy, except it was then interrupted by the news that the Bastard's father had died, and also the plague was back. The sports fans then left and spread it all over the country.

This event further alienated Warwick, who was in France meeting with Louis the Spider, Burgundy's rival.

The worst Woodville outrage came following one of the numerous plots against the king. In June 1468, the authorities arrested a shoemaker, John Cornelius, a servant of a well-known Lancastrian. Cornelius was returning to Queen Margaret after allegedly delivering letters to supporters and was seized in London; he spent three days in the Tower where he was tortured by burning his feet 'until he confessed many things' (feet burning would be followed by stripping off the flesh using red-hot pincers, at which point most people would admit to anything). Among those he named was John Hawkins, a servant of Warwick's friend Lord Wenlock, who was set up on the rack and accused one Sir Thomas Cook of being part of the plot.

Cook was a wealthy London merchant with a sumptuous house and Jacquetta, the queen's mother, took a liking to a tapestry he owned. It was 'wrought in most richest wise with gold of the whole story of the siege of Jerusalem' and cost eight hundred pounds, a fortune equivalent to one million dollars today. She used an old law called 'Queen's Gold' to demand that Cook sell the tapestry to her for far less than its value, but he refused. The Woodvilles then accused him of working for the Lancastrians, and sent retainers to sack his houses in London and the country. Rivers had Cook tried with 'misprision of treason' for not disclosing a loan he had made to

Margaret's agent many years before; they gave him a fine of eight thousand pounds and he was ruined.

There were other plots; Richard Steeres, a former servant of Exeter and member of the Skinners' Company—one of London's guilds—and 'one of the cunningest players of the tennis in England,' was caught with letters from Margaret. London alderman Sir John Plummer and sheriff Humphrey Haurford were also accused of plotting against the king, while the heirs to the Courtenay and Hungerford families were executed for treason in early 1469. There was a general atmosphere of paranoia.

And Warwick was upset by further matches orchestrated by the Woodville clan; the queen's son Thomas Grey married the king's niece Anne Holland, heiress of the Duke of Exeter, even though Warwick's nephew had been offered the match. Edward alienated his cousin by removing from his brother Archbishop George Neville the ceremonial Great Seal held by archbishops of York, a public sign of disfavor. Warwick, away in Burgundy, was furious when he learned about it. It got to such a state in their relationship that the king ignored Warwick when he came to court with his French allies, and by January 1468, Warwick had returned to his northern estates and refused to attend the King's Council being held at Coventry if Earl Rivers, Lord Scales, and Lord Herbert were there. And so the Kingmaker now decided to seize power, one way or the other.

CHAPTER NINE

Let Me Embrace Thee, Sweet Adversity

In 1466, the bones of Thomas of Lancaster at Pontefract Castle in Yorkshire were rumored to be sweating, seen as a sign of Edward's unpopularity; Thomas had been executed by his cousin Edward II in 1322 and his burial place had become a shrine to opponents of the king. It was a sign of increased agitation, as well as increasing crime: the Parliament of 1467 implored the king to deal with 'homicides, murders, riots, extortions, rapes of women, robberies, and other crimes which had been habitually and lamentably committed and perpetrated throughout the realm.'

However, the real troubles started in the spring of 1469, with two separate risings in Yorkshire, led by two men, both of them called Robin, one of whom was clearly put up to it by Warwick. Robin Mend-all, also known as Robin of Redesdale, had named himself in tribute to Robin Hood, legendary outlaw in the north Midlands, and he was most likely Sir John Conyers, a cousin by marriage of Warwick. Meanwhile, a second unconnected uprising took place in the east of the county, led by a Robin of Holderness. The Redesdale rebels said they were saving the king from 'the deceiving covetous rule and guiding of certain

seducious persons' (i.e., the Woodvilles and Edward's other cronies), who 'caused our said sovereign lord and his realm to fall in
great poverty of misery, disturbing the ministration of the laws,
only intending to their own promotion and enriching.' The riots
were put down by Warwick's brother John Neville, although he
may have allowed the ringleaders to go free and a second uprising was clearly sponsored by the Nevilles. There were rumors of
sixty thousand people involved in this 'great insurrection' and
'whirlwind from the north.'

King Edward headed north in mid-June along with Gloucester,
Rivers, Scales, and other Woodvilles, but as he did so the realization
of how serious it could be began to sink in, and he called up more
men. The king also wrote to Warwick, Clarence, and George Neville, but they replied that they were headed to Calais for a 'wedding,'
so conveniently weren't able to help. However, the following day,
July 12, Warwick and his confederates wrote an open letter to the
king supporting the uprising, and accusing the Woodvilles as well
as William Herbert, Humphrey Stafford, and others of letting the
kingdom 'fall in great poverty of misery.'

Warwick had now formed an alliance with the king's shallow
brother George, Duke of Clarence. George was born with good
looks like Edward—tall, blond, handsome—and shared his cruel
and violent streak, too, but he was also impulsive, vain, and foolish.
He seemed to lack any sense of maturity or self-control, and was easily flattered and tempted into unwise decisions.

Clarence had been recognized as an adult in 1466 when he was
sixteen and given huge estates in Staffordshire in the midlands; he
had the most lavish household staff in England, a retinue of four
hundred people at an annual cost of forty-five hundred pounds and a
court larger than the king's. Frustrated that all the eligible men had
been taken by Woodville girls, Warwick approached Clarence and
proposed that his daughter Isabel should marry him, even though
they were closely related; Edward blocked the plan, as Warwick and

Clarence were now the biggest lords in the midlands, and combined they would be a threat.

The rebels now headed south to join up with Warwick and Clarence, but at Edgecote Moor in Oxfordshire, they met a royal force, who defeated them. The Earl of Pembroke, Edward's ruler in Wales, and his brother Sir Richard Herbert were captured, and Warwick had them beheaded after a sham trial. Edward IV was then taken prisoner by a group led by George Neville, meaning there were now two kings in their custody. Warwick had effectively taken over in a coup, and sent out his agents to capture the queen's father and brother Sir John Woodville—he had them beheaded in Coventry, and so poor Catherine Neville found herself widowed for the fourth time. Warwick then had Earl Rivers's wife Jacquetta arrested on witchcraft charges, accusing her of using black arts to get her daughter married to the king. A neighbor, Thomas Wake, produced two small lead figures, which were supposed to represent the king and queen, along with another of a 'man of arms,' broken in the middle and with wire wrapped around it. Although it's fair to say that most people were quite credulous at the time, such was the strength of the English judiciary that had been established in the previous centuries that even in times of tyranny and madness, judges and juries could not be bullied; she was found not guilty.

Warwick's authority was at any rate falling to pieces. Humphrey Neville, from a different branch of the enormous family, began a rebellion in the North in August, raising Henry VI's banners, which Warwick was able to easily beat, having the leader brought back to London to be beheaded. But such was the anarchy in London that by October 1469, Warwick was forced to release Edward, who arrived in the city with Gloucester, Suffolk, Hastings, the London mayor, city aldermen, two hundred guild members, and one thousand horses. Edward was magnanimous and spoke of Warwick and his gang as 'his best friends,' but after he had killed his father-in-law and brother-in-law, it was clear things were never going to be exactly the same again.

Edward now promoted the few people he could trust, chiefly his youngest brother Richard, Duke of Gloucester. Just seventeen, Richard was made constable of England, and justiciar and steward of Wales, all important roles. Richard Gloucester, as he styled himself, was the very opposite of his two brothers, strongly resembling their father with his dark hair and pale skin, and with a frail, feminine physique; he also had a deformity in his spine that made him appear far shorter, and which caused him constant pain throughout his life. Over the coming years, he would become his brother's right-hand man.

Edward wanted to weaken the Nevilles and rebalance power in the North. Although John Neville had remained loyal, the king released the latest Henry Percy from imprisonment and made him Earl of Northumberland again; instead, John Neville was given land in the Southwest, while Neville's son George was made Duke of Bedford and betrothed to Elizabeth of York, the king's eldest daughter.

Warwick's plan to rule with Edward as a pawn had failed, so he now instigated Plan B, an ill-thought-out scheme to place Clarence on the throne. In March 1470, there was a rebellion in Lincolnshire, beginning as a feud between two local men, Lord Welles and Sir Thomas Burgh, which snowballed into something bigger. On March 12, 1470, in Stamford, the king destroyed them in a very short, one-sided battle, with the rebels throwing off their coats to get away, giving it the name Losecoat Field. And so Warwick and Clarence fled from the South Coast to France, and when the king arrived in Exeter, he noticed that the guildhall there displayed the ragged staff badge of Warwick, and so the king left his sword as a reminder of where power really lay. Both are still at Exeter.

The king, meanwhile, recalled his lord high executioner, John Tiptoft, from Ireland. If there was a television series about the war, Tiptoft is the role every actor would relish playing.[64] A refined and cultured Renaissance man, the Earl of Worcester owned a rarefied collection of books and had made pilgrimages to Jerusalem.

Considered 'the greatest English humanist of his time,' Tiptoft had traveled to Rome, Venice, and Padua, and spent his three years in Italy collecting rare books and learning from Renaissance princes. After two years at Padua, he 'returned to England with a precarious cargo of manuscripts—Lucretius, Suetonius, Tacitus, Sallust, and others,' and was an enthusiastic scholar and translator of Latin and Italian classics, among them Bounaccorso da Montemagno's *Controversia de Nobilitate*. He had studied law at the university of Padua and, in 1460, delivered an oration before the pope that was supposed to be so beautiful that the Holy Father was reduced to tears.

He was also a sadist of unimaginable cruelty, who really, really enjoyed the role of executioner. On top of hanging and drawing and quartering a number of people through the years, including the Earl of Oxford and his son, he also introduced impaling to England, a Balkan practice that horrified even the London mob, who had pretty high tolerance levels for that sort of thing. In March, after the king had sent the new Earl Rivers to capture Warwick's ship in Southampton, he arranged for Tiptoft to sit in judgment on the captive men. The executioner took twenty 'gentlemen and yeomen' affiliates of Warwick and had them drawn, quartered, and impaled in public, to widespread horror; sharpened stakes were forced between their buttocks and their heads stuck onto the polls protruding out of the other end. Medieval crowds loved a good painful execution but even this was a bit much for them, so as a result, contemporary John Warkworth wrote, the Earl became 'greatly behated among the people.'[65]

Warwick and Clarence fled to Calais but were denied entry by the garrison there, and while at sea Clarence's wife Isabel went into labor, but the baby was stillborn. Instead, the wind pushed them in the direction of France where, along the way, Warwick had increased his fleet by seizing a number of Flemish and Dutch ships en route, arriving at Honfleur at the end of the month. This kind of thing made him hugely popular as the general public loved a bit of piracy if it was their people doing it against foreigners; Warwick now had a fleet of ten ships, compared to the English navy that was down to just one.

It was in France that Warwick now came up with Plan C, an unlikely alliance with Queen Margaret, who was in Koeur, a castle to the east of Paris.

He had deposed her husband. He had slandered her. He had tried to disinherit her son. Now, in a meeting arranged by French King Louis the Spider, Warwick went to see Margaret at Angers on July 22—where she kept him on his knees for fifteen minutes before she would let him stand up again. He also promised to kneel before her at Westminster when they got back. When she met Warwick 'the said queen was right difficile,' it was reported, rather understandably. Still, she agreed that her son Edward would marry his younger daughter Anne, a plan that was inevitably going to end in tears. The French ambassador Commynes wrote of Lady Anne and Edward of Westminster: 'That was a strange marriage. Warwick had defeated and ruined the prince's father, and now he made him marry his daughter.' The two were also closely related, but Louis the Spider stumped up the necessary bribe for a papal dispensation.

Edward and Anne Neville were joined in holy matrimony on July 25, 1470, in Normandy; but in fact, Margaret had forbidden her son to consummate his marriage so when the time came, he could find a more suitable bride. Which was just as well, for while Anne was 'seemly, amiable, and beauteous, right virtuous and full gracious,' Edward of Westminster had developed into a sadist at a very early age. A Milanese envoy in 1467 recalled that the thirteen-year-old, who had grown up in an atmosphere of extreme violence, 'already talks of nothing but cutting off heads or making war, as if he had everything in his hands or was the god of battle.'

Warwick, Clarence, and the ultra-loyal Lancastrians Jasper Tudor and John de Vere set sail from Normandy on September 9, 1470, and landed after four days in Devon, announcing the restoration of

Henry VI. Edward was in the midlands at the time, and soon found out that Warwick's brother John Neville had sided with the rebels, as had Lord Stanley. He then learned that even his brother George, Duke of Clarence had also joined the rebellion. Edward was in bed in Doncaster when his minstrel burst in and told him his enemies were only six or seven miles away; he was forced to flee to Burgundy with his brother Richard, Lord Hastings, and Earl Rivers, so poor that he had to pay for the crossing by selling his fur-lined coat.

Queen Elizabeth and her children stayed in Westminster while Londoners closed the walls to Warwick's French mercenaries, but could do nothing when, on October 6, Warwick and Clarence rode in and released Henry VI, 'now a permanent imbecile,' from captivity. According to Henry's confessor John Blacman, the king had 'patiently endured hunger, thirst, mockings, derisions, abuse, and many other hardships.' Although Henry was restored, all the lords and knights present wore the badge of Warwick.

Warwick planned to be conciliatory toward defeated Yorkists, but he would make an exemption for Tiptoft, who was captured hiding up a tree near Huntingdon. Young John de Vere, whose father and brother had been killed by the hated Earl of Worcester, presided over his trial and in front of an enormous braying London mob; the executioner was executed in style, wearing his best clothes and telling the axmen to do it in three strokes.

Warwick declared that Edward was a bastard, using the old rumor that his real father was a Norman archer, a pretty unlikely story that nonetheless made George heir presumptive, after Edward of Westminster. On November 2, meanwhile, Elizabeth Woodville gave birth to a son, yet another Edward, in London, and Henry VI sent for a midwife and provided her with beef, a great kindness typical of the man. In a grisly twist of fate, the baby and the gentle king would both one day be murdered by the same man.

Archbishop Neville tried to arouse sympathy for King Henry by making him parade through the streets of the city, but 'his shabby, feeble-witted appearance only alienated support.' The London mob were shocked by how badly dressed he was, in an old gown, and a witness, George Chastellain, described him as 'a stuffed wool sack lifted by its ears, a shadow on the wall, bandied about as in a game of blind man's bluff . . . submissive and mute, like a crowned calf.' Not an inspiring leader, then.

Warwick now publicly praised 'the most noble Princess Margaret, queen of England' to rescue 'our most dread sovereign lord, King Henry VI' from 'his great rebel and enemy, Edward, late Earl of March, usurper, oppressor, and destroyer of our said sovereign lord and of the noble blood of all the realm of England and of the good, true commons of the same.' So everyone was friends, except that they all hated one another and there were obviously problems with this new alliance. On top of all the bad blood, Warwick, Clarence, and others had gained lands at the expense of the Cliffords, Courtenays, Somersets, and Tudors. Would they now have to give it all back?

Barnet and Tewkesbury

Things looked desperate for Edward, although the usurped usurper was not finished yet. In September 1470, Duke Charles of Burgundy had allowed him to stay but he was not very welcome; Charles sent friendly messages to the new regime through the Duke of Exeter, who had become a sort of down-and-out in Bruges.

However, in February 1471, Duke Charles changed his mind after it became clear that Warwick was going to support Louis in a war against him. He lent Edward some money and troops, although a very small amount; he set sail with at most fifteen hundred Englishmen and three hundred Flemish mercenaries, and he had also obtained ships from the Hanseatic League, the collection of mostly German city-states across the sea. It was a pathetic force, and as an Italian commented, the king who left by the door was attempting to reenter through the window.

Edward landed at Ravenspur, the same spot in Yorkshire where Henry IV had arrived in 1399 and, like him, claimed—improbably—that he was only back to reclaim his private lands. It was quite a risk, as with his tiny force he was entirely at the mercy of the new Earl of Northumberland; the Percys, however, had had enough of war, and the latest Earl was actually sympathetic to Edward but knew he could not get northern men to fight for the victor of Towton, especially as Yorkshire, despite its name, was heavily Lancastrian. So he just let Edward through.

Edward first walked into York, bearing Henry's banners in an obviously disingenuous sign of loyalty, and then headed south toward Tadcaster, Wakefield, Doncaster, Nottingham, and Leicester. Marching with four thousand men, he met Sir William Stanley's army of two thousand; the Stanleys, notoriously, never sided with anyone who might lose. At Northampton in 1460, his brother Thomas Stanley had ignored the king's summons because he wished to see which way the wind blew. This time they went with Edward.

On March 29, Edward reached Coventry, and Warwick retreated inside the walls. Clarence was in the Southwest and was headed in their direction; however, Clarence's wife was 'no fool,' as a contemporary said, and was persuaded by a lady-in-waiting that this alliance was going nowhere, and that her husband would stand no chance so long as Edward of Westminster was heir. When Edward came across Clarence's four thousand men near Banbury, their younger brother Richard was sent to talk him over, which he did, adding his men to the king's. What the common soldiers thought about this is not recorded, nor did anyone probably care.

Henry was put on procession a second time for the people of London in April 9, 1471, but he was so pathetic he had to have his hand held by Archbishop Neville while he sat limply on his horse and was dressed in 'a long blue gown of velvet as though he had no more to change with,' as one observer noted.

As Edward approached London, the mayor, John Stockton, showed true leadership in the face of a difficult situation by taking to his bed and pretending to be sick. The merchants of the capital had lent Edward a lot of money and so many wanted him back anyway; Commynes also suggested that Edward had support from the city because the 'wives of rich citizens with whom he had been closely and secretly acquainted, won over their husbands and relations to his cause.' The city aldermen told their troops to go home and have dinner, and in the night the Yorkists took over.

And so Edward entered London unopposed on April 11, and there he met his son for the first time, while Henry VI greeted him with the words: 'Cousin Edward, I am right glad to see you. I hold my life in no danger from your hands.' Which turned out to be a rather optimistic view.

There followed the Battle of Barnet three days later on Easter Sunday, at a place called Dead Man's Bottom, continuing the tradition of poetically named battle sites. Edward turned up with ten thousand men, and poor King Henry was once again a prisoner. Edward and Gloucester fought their cousins Warwick and Montagu and brother-in-law Exeter, while Hastings was pitted against his brothers-in-law Oxford and the Nevilles. As for the common troops, Commynes reported that 'when he left Flanders, King Edward made up his mind that he was not going to keep his old custom of shouting "spare the commons and kill the gentles" as he had during earlier battles because he had developed a deep hatred for ordinary English people on account of the Earl of Warwick being so popular with them.'

The battle was like a scrum, except that the two armies were not lined up correctly and so each side had a flank overshot, causing the mass of men to move in a counterclockwise direction. It looked like Warwick might beat his cousin, and some of Edward's men had already run back to London and spread the rumor he had lost. However, just as he won Towton because of the wind and snow, here the dismal British weather came to Edward's aid once again; in the thick fog, Warwick's affinity mistook the Lancastrian Earl of Oxford's banner of an Enrayed Star for Edward's Sun in Splendor, and fired at them, thinking they had switched sides, and Oxford's men ran off shouting 'treason!'

The Battle of Barnet was over by 8 a.m., by which point there were ten thousand spent arrows on the battlefield. The Duke of Exeter was left for dead, but eventually reached the sanctuary at Westminster; he had been knocked unconscious but was saved by a servant. Oxford was the only Lancastrian to escape unhurt. Warwick tried to get away but was recognized by his ostentatious and colorful blazoned coat and beaten to death by a group of soldiers, although the king had wanted him alive. His brother Montagu, who had distinguished himself on the day by 'slicing off heads and limbs from everyone whom he encountered,' was also killed and their bodies were displayed at St. Paul's Cathedral to prove to the common people that they were indeed dead.

Sir John Paston (II), who fought for the Earl of Oxford, wrote afterwards that 'the world is right queasy.' His brother John (III) received an arrow wound in the arm, but both survived.

Meanwhile, Margaret and her son Edward had not crossed the channel until they were quite sure it was safe to do so, and chose to arrive to their newly restored kingdom less than twenty-four hours before their ally Warwick was killed, so they had to face Edward alone.

The victor of Barnet now issued proclamations against 'Margaret calling herself Queen, which is a Frenchwoman born and daughter to him that is extreme adversary and mortal enemy to all this our land.' The Yorkists intercepted Margaret's forces in the West on May 4, the enemy now a tired and desolate body of men who had walked forty-five miles without rest. The Lancastrians had encamped south of Tewkesbury: in front of them were 'foul lanes and deep dykes, and many hedges with hills and valleys . . . as evil a place to approach as could possibly have been devised.' However, it was not enough to save them, and Edward was once again the winner.

It was finally the moment Henry VI's crazed son, Edward of Westminster, had looked forward to, having 'applied himself wholly to feats of arms, much delighting to ride upon wild and unbroken horses, not sparing with spurs to fierceness . . . he practised also sometimes with the poke, sometimes with the sword.' However, it didn't go well for the young psychopath and, wearing a coat with the arms of England, he was killed, along with two thousand others. Even amid the battle, such were the hatreds that had overcome the aristocracy that the Duke of Somerset killed fellow Lancastrian Lord Wenlock by smashing his brains out with a battle-ax, accusing him of not being supportive enough.

Afterward, Somerset sheltered at Tewkesbury Abbey, which as a sanctuary he was supposed to be safe in, but two days later he, Courtenay, and some others were taken out and beheaded; the third Somerset to die in the war and the third of three Courtenay brothers to be killed. Somerset's younger brother John was also killed in the battle and so the family became extinct. After Tewkesbury, men who had switched sides were executed on Edward's orders; however, those who had always fought for the Lancastrians, like John Fortescue, were given a pardon.

Almost all opposition was now over, except for Thomas Neville, an illegitimate son of Edward's uncle known as 'the Bastard of Fauconberg,' who still controlled an army in Kent from which to attack London; he destroyed parts of the bridge, but the city was defended well by Earl Rivers, and the bastard escaped to France. He was later captured at Southampton, and his head placed on London Bridge. Afterward, numerous rebels were executed, although more were fined: 'Such as were rich were hanged by the purse, and the others that were needy were hanged by the neck.'

Among the few survivors were Henry VI's half brother Jasper Tudor and his young nephew Henry, who in June arrived in Brittany after being blown off course, which was lucky as the French would have sold them to Edward. Duke Francis of Brittany made them his prisoners, and had them separated and placed with Breton guards.

King Edward reentered London once again on May 21 at the head of a victory procession; at the very back, in a cart, was Queen Margaret, a broken woman who would endure the next four years a prisoner of her former lady-in-waiting, Alice de la Pole. Eventually, she was ransomed back to Louis XI and her remaining life was spent miserably in France, surviving on a tiny pension until her death in 1482; she did not leave enough money afterward to pay off her debts or give her servants anything. Margaret had never been popular, although her determination in fighting for her son, despite her husband being simpleminded, earned her some respect. As one contemporary said, she was 'more wittier than the king,' though in fairness that was a fairly low bar.

Ambassador Sforza de' Bettini, contemplating from his ambassadorial post in France the difficulty of finding reliable information about England to send to his master in Milan, rather summed up the mood when he said: 'I wish the country and the people were plunged deep in the sea because of their lack of stability, for I feel like one going to the torture when I write about them, and no one ever hears twice alike about English affairs.'

Henry VI wasn't for this world much longer, and his last few days were filled with visions, one in which he saw a woman try to drown a child. After his heir's death, Henry himself became expendable, and a few days later he died of 'pure displeasure and melancholy,' according to official reports, although his head had been smashed in, which would certainly cause most people some displeasure. Possibly, he was maced to death by Richard of Gloucester, between the hours of eleven and midnight;[66] *The Great Chronicle of London*, a collection of diaries by London merchants, stated that of Henry VI's death 'The most common fame then went that the Duke of Gloucester was not all guiltless.' When the king's body was exhumed in 1910 it was found that his skull was matted with blood, suggesting he had been hit over the head.

His torment was at last over, for as Henry VI had once said: 'kingdoms are but cares.' The House of Lancaster was finished, and even one of the most loyal of Henry's followers, the leading church-man John Morton, now changed sides. He explained that while he wanted the Lancastrians to win, 'But after that God had ordered him to lose it, and King Edward to reign, I was never so mad that I would with a dead man strive against the quick.' The War of the Roses was finally over. Or so it seemed.

CHAPTER TEN

False, Fleeting, Perjur'd Clarence

Bruges, where Edward had stayed in exile, was known as the Venice of the North, and was culturally more advanced than England. The Duke of Burgundy had the finest library in Europe—'gorgeously illuminated manuscripts bound in gem-crusted covers'—while his wife, Edward's sister Margaret, was a devoted fan of romance stories. In 1469, she asked an English-born businessman called William Caxton to translate a *History of Troy* for her; Caxton was a mercer—an exporter of wool—and may have helped Edward with loans for arms during his exile, but he was also an avid reader and spoke several languages, and unusually for a trader, spent his spare time translating books. When he had finished writing out the 210,000-word epic for Margaret, he was exhausted and heavily regretted having promised several copies to friends already.

Luckily, two years later, during a business trip to Cologne, Caxton discovered a revolutionary new invention that would make this a lot easier—printing. He was fifty-one when he started out in his groundbreaking second career for which he became forever famous.

Printing had been invented in Germany by a goldsmith and metal merchant from Mainz called Johannes Guttenberg (he was baptized Johannes Gensfleisch, which means 'gooseflesh,' so he used his mother's maiden name instead). In 1439, Guttenberg, then in his forties, had been involved in a financial disaster after making a number of polished metal mirrors that supposedly captured holy light from religious relics, to sell to pilgrims in Aachen, the resting place of the Emperor Charlemagne. However, because of flooding, the planned festival never went ahead, and since insurance hadn't been invented, he was unable to repay investors.

Desperate, he now promised to find the money with a 'secret'; normally when people say this, it's a sign they're never going to repay you and you'll probably never see them again, but Guttenberg was German, and he did actually have a secret, an invention called movable type, which he'd developed from 'punchcutting,' the process of making coins. Five years later, while living in Strasbourg, Guttenberg had completed his new technology, and by 1448, his printing press was ready. In 1453, the same year the English were driven out of France and Constantinople fell to the Ottomans, the first Bible was printed in Mainz; within twenty years, over one hundred printing presses were across western Europe, of which half were in Italy.

Printing was to have a revolutionary influence, allowing men (and eventually women) outside of the aristocracy and priesthood power that a century before was unimaginable, and to spread new ideas—although not necessarily more rational ones. Among the earliest and most popular books was *Malleus Maleficarum*, which helped to popularize the craze for witchcraft among a gullible public.

In 1475, Caxton published the first book printed in English, *Recuyell of the Histories of Troy*, followed the same year by *The Game and Playe of Chesse*, as well as the first book printed in French. Another, *The Dictes and Sayenges of the Phylosophers*, was translated by the queen's brother, now Earl Rivers, and caused an outcry by reprinting some of Socrates's women-hating rants; Caxton added as a postscript, in the style of a celebrity who has unwittingly offended some group, that it didn't apply to England as 'the women of this country be right, good, wise, pleasant, humble, discreet, sober, chaste, and obedient to their husbands, true, secret, steadfast, ever busy and never idle, temperate in speaking, and virtuous in all their works.' King Edward also sponsored Caxton, and, being interested in history, he kept a copy of *The Life of Caesar*.

Caxton's printing also led to the standardization of the English language, since before then people in neighboring counties could scarcely understand one another. For example, Englishmen from the Southwest said, 'I be, thee bis, he baint,' rather than 'I am, you are, he is,' and continued to speak this way until the late nineteenth century, as anyone forced to read Thomas Hardy at school will know (this archaic way of talking is of course related to German, for which the equivalent is *Ich bin, du bis, er bist*). Caxton made spelling uniform, using East Midlands English as the standard, a rather misleading name as it refers to the dialect between London, Oxford, and Cambridge. Sometimes the spelling of one region would be made the standard while the pronunciation of another became more common, which is why to people learning English, its spelling makes absolutely no sense ('rough' rhymes with 'tough' but not 'dough'). 'Busy' ended up being pronounced in the London fashion, while bury was pronounced the Kentish way, but neither was spelled in that dialect. The northern 'loves' won out over the Kentish 'loveth' or London 'loven,' although a few unusual words continued to be spelled in the latter style—children, brethren, and oxen. Printing also came about during the Great Vowel Shift, when English pronunciation changed considerably, previously sounding a lot more like Danish; until then, knee, lamb, laugh, gnaw, and night were pronounced as they were spelt. To make matters more confusing, many printers were from the Netherlands and so Dutch spellings of words such as ghost or gherkin were adopted, despite making no sense.

In 1476, Caxton started his printing press by Westminster Abbey, which is why printing unions called themselves 'chapels' until the late twentieth century. Caxton became rich as the new craze took off, though some aristocrats at the time still thought printing vulgar, and employed professional writers to copy out books for their drawing rooms, clearly unwilling to accept the inevitable. When the great printer died in 1491, he left his business to his assistant, the aptly named Jan Wynkyn de Worde, who, in 1500, moved the press to Fleet Street, which for the next five centuries became the home of British journalism; the last two journalists left the 'Street of Shame' only in 2016.[67] Nearby is Paternoster Row, close to St. Paul's cathedral, where a number of legal scriveners began to congregate from 1400, further helping to standardize the language; by 1470, there were one thousand legal students in England, several times what there had been a century before.

Invasion of France, sort of

The king was still broke, so poor that in 1475 he resorted to 'benevolences,' a system of raising money where rich men were summoned to one-on-one interviews where Edward charmed them into giving him cash, with a tiny undertone of menace; he also kissed their wives in front of them in an overly courteous but also slightly unnerving way. Edward even went on a tour of England trying to get money, although he soon hit upon an even better scheme.

Kings of England at the time were expected to make war abroad, especially in France, as it was seen as the only way to unite the country and gain popularity; it didn't matter that it was nonsensical, it was just what they did. Edward liked the idea in theory, but by now he was becoming increasingly fat and lazy and would rather spend his evenings feasting with buxom wenches. In July 1475, however, the king agreed to invade France with ten thousand men, and a royal spokesman in the Commons suggested that war would lower crime as unruly elements would go abroad.

And so an English army arrived in Calais, then marched aimlessly around Picardy and Artois, where they settled in Amiens, but there didn't seem to be much fight in the English. The invasion force of 1475 was a rabble compared to previous ones, and diplomat Philippe de Commynes wrote, 'I don't exaggerate when I say that Edward's men seemed very inexperienced and unused to active service, since they rode in such ragged order.' At Amiens, the gates were left open and the French soldiers outside and the English inside passed to and fro, and began to organize jousting and archery tournaments. They even drank together with no sign of any problems. Edward sent letters to the King of France making a token demand of the return of the Plantagenet lands, a totally ridiculous request that he had no intention of pushing, but after some haggling this was watered down to a seventy-five thousand crowns bribe and an annual payment of fifty thousand.

The two kings agreed to meet on the River Somme on August 29, in a special room that had to be built in the middle of the bridge to prevent any assassinations (after what had happened to the Duke of Burgundy back in 1419). Edward, who was always at ease with foreigners and spoke fluent French—he was born in Normandy and was close to his Norman nanny—got on like a house on fire with Louis. After giving a down payment, the French organized drinks for their guests, so that it was said that when the English army went to France 'not a drop of water was drunk.'

Two long tables were placed on each side of the street and vast amounts of wine were produced. 'At both tables the king had sat five or six boon companions, fat and sleek noblemen, to welcome any Englishman who felt like having a cheerful glass . . . nine or ten taverns were generously supplied with anything they wanted, where they could have whatever they ordered without paying for it, by command of the king of France who paid the entire cost of the entertainment which went on for three or four days.' Commynes visited one tavern at 9 a.m. where he found vast quantities had already been drunk; the place was full of Englishmen 'some of whom were singing, others asleep and all of them very drunk.' Even King Edward, who was no Mother Teresa on matters moral, was so ashamed of the troops that he had many thrown out of the city.

Louis XI had also arranged for prostitutes to entertain the troops, and it was observed that 'many a man was lost that fell to the lust of women, who were burnt by them; and their members rotted away and they died.' Afterwards, the French king said: 'I have chased the English out of France more easily than my father did, for he had to drive them out with armies, while I have seen them off with venison and good French wine.'

Duke Charles of Burgundy was apparently so angry at this peace deal that he ate his ribbon of the garter, or at least tore it with his teeth. He wasn't the only one; the king's excitable younger brother Gloucester, keen to have a war with the French, publicly made his feelings known about the peace. However, for King Edward it was all a bit of a jolly jaunt, and a hugely profitable one too, and on the way home he topped it off by having his brother-in-law the Duke of Exeter thrown overboard. This is at least the popular story—the former torturer, who had been brought along as a prisoner, certainly died en route, although at a time when sea travel was hazardous, boats rickety, and swimming rare, many died at sea.

Clarence

Another former rebel, Edward's brother Clarence, had been forgiven after 1471, and allowed to have his wife Isabel Neville's lands, which she'd inherited from her father Warwick, and yet he remained in conflict with his younger brother. Gloucester had chosen to marry Anne Neville, Isabel's sister and the widow of Edward of Westminster, but Clarence wanted all the inheritance to himself and so kidnapped her and had her disguised as a maid at one of his castles. Gloucester managed to rescue her, although as it transpires she probably would have been better off as a nun.

However, the two brothers could at least agree, in 1474, to have Warwick's wife declared legally dead so they could get her land, even though she was quite clearly alive. Gloucester showed other signs of ruthlessness: in Christmas 1472, he sent sixteen men to Bromley Priory at Stratford-le-Bow, east of London, to abduct the seventy-year-old dowager Countess of Oxford, the elderly mother of the Earl of Oxford, who was dragged through the snow by his men. Richard, 'acting of his insatiable covetise' obtained her estates illegally 'by great threats and heinous menace of loss of life.' The Duke told the old lady she would lose all her estates, and, terrified, she was brought to another house in London and bullied into signing over her land to Richard.

Clarence and Edward, meanwhile, looked upon each other 'with no very fraternal eyes,' and, in October 1476, George seems to have lost his mind after his wife died during childbirth. The Duke turned up in Somerset and blamed a local widow, Ankarette Twynho, for her death, accusing her of being a witch; Twynho was charged with sorcery and of poisoning the Lady Isabel, to whom she was once lady-in-waiting, by serving her 'a venomous drink of ale mixed with poison.' A mob of some eighty 'riotous and misgoverned persons' loyal to Clarence seized the poor woman, who was dragged through the streets of Warwick and hanged. Then a Warwickshire man called John Thirsby was also strung up for killing Clarence's stillborn son and another knight, Sir Roger Tucotes, was accused, but escaped to London to report the incident.

Clarence had told friends that Edward used magic to rule, and 'wrought by necromancy . . . [he] . . . used craft to poison his subjects.' As it turned out, however, Clarence had been employing warlocks himself: John Stacey, who was an astronomy expert at Merton College, had admitted under torture to having tried to kill a nobleman, Lord Beauchamp, at his wife's instigation by melting a laden image. He had also implied that one of Clarence's household was involved in 'imagining' the death of King Edward; Stacey, along with two other men, Thomas Blake and Thomas Budret, was also accused of circulating 'bills, rhymes, and ballads' critical of the monarch.

Clarence was brought before the king, where he made things much worse by repeating the allegation of necromancy and claiming that the king was a bastard. The 'incorrigible' prince, as the king called his brother, was charged with treason and put to death, supposedly drowned in a vat of sweet wine, the end of 'false, fleeting, perjur'd Clarence.'

This was all stirred up by the wily French king, who was trying to drive a wedge between Edward IV and his sister Margaret of Burgundy, and so got the French ambassador to subtly imply that Margaret was trying to marry her stepdaughter to Clarence. On top of this, a soothsayer had apparently told King Edward that 'G' would take his crown, and this may have fueled his paranoia about George Clarence; after all, his other brother Richard of Gloucester would never do anything bad.

As it was, Edward IV had also employed the services of a necromancer, one Friar Bungay, to shroud the battlefield of Barnet in mist and to stir up storms, so everyone was at it.

The king's last few years were a boom time for the economy, but Edward got fatter and more grotesque, gorging himself slowly to death while continuing to womanize; he had now become so degenerate that he would purge his stomach so he could eat again. His favorite mistress—hated by the queen—was Jane Shore, the daughter of John Lambert, a member of Mercers Company and part of London's wealthy mercantile class. John Lambert had been apprenticed in 1436 to Thomas Onehand, one of the numerous strangely named figures from the period. Jane, confusingly also called Elizabeth, had been divorced because of her husband's impotence, and had had to get a letter from Pope Sixtus mandating that she was living with William Shore 'but that he is so frigid and impotent that she, desirous of being a mother and having offspring, requested over and over again' to end the marriage, which was duly annulled. All of this was done publicly—how Mr. Shore must have longed for a system of no-fault divorce.

The king certainly didn't have any problems in that department, and Jane Shore played an important role in English history—Edward was going to abolish Eton, the school for poor boys set up by Henry VI, but the compassionate 'Mr. Shore's wife' persuaded him otherwise, and after 1471 he visited three times. Of the fifty-six British prime ministers at the time of writing, nineteen went to Eton.

Uniquely, Edward did not pass on 'Shore's wife' to his cronies and had great affection for her. So, however, did Hastings, who seems to have been in love with her; Hastings, despite being married to Warwick's sister Katherine, had remained loyal to Edward in 1470 and fought at Barnet and Tewkesbury, and afterwards was put in charge of Calais. Unfortunately, he had become deadly enemies with Edward's stepson, Thomas Grey, who became Marquess of Dorset in 1475, and was given land in Devon and Cornwall. Hastings and Grey were at war with each other, their feud having started over 'the mistresses whom they had abducted or had tried to entice away from each other,' but it also involved land.

King Edward was now trying to connect his family to the entire nobility to ensure there were no more uprisings. He married his second son, Richard, to Anne, the daughter of the Duke of Norfolk, even though Richard was just four and his wife five. The marriage took place on January 15, 1478, and after the ceremony, Gloucester dipped into golden basins filled with coins 'and threw a largesse to the onlookers.' Sadly, Anne died just four years later making Richard a widow at eight.

Gloucester was put in charge of the dangerous former Neville territory in the North, and he also got Richmond, a prize possession in Yorkshire. Richard became effectively king of the North, and sickened by the Woodvilles, whom he had grown to hate with a passion, he retreated to his own heartland around Middleham in Yorkshire.

And it was left to Richard to fight off the Scots after conflict erupted again on the border, stirred up when Louis XI had persuaded Scotland's weak-willed James III to start a war in 1479–1480. The unintended consequence was England's first royal postal system, as Edward, in 1482, established relays of horsemen at every twenty miles stabled to carry dispatches from London to the Scottish borders at the rate of one hundred miles per day, three times the previous speed. The aim was to make rebellions and Scottish invasions easier to tackle; at the time, communication was so bad that by the time, the authorities in London learned about an uprising in the North, it might already have snowballed.

Gloucester raised an army of twenty thousand and took the border town of Berwick during his 1482–3 campaign and, as a result, in January he was given his own palatinate in Westmorland and Cumberland. Increasingly, Edward turned to his brother for advice and support, and when a new tax was imposed in 1483, Richard's four northern counties were exempt. Meanwhile, France had attacked Burgundy, but Edward didn't help, hoping that Louis would die soon, as he had already had two attacks of apoplexy. This didn't work and Burgundy was half-swallowed up by France, and the daughter of the Duke married the dauphin, even though he had been supposed to marry Edward's eldest daughter. The Yorkist foreign policy ended in failure.

The king, once so dynamic and youthful, had grown fat and tired, gorged on wine and food. Aged just forty, he became seriously ill during Easter 1483 after going fishing on the Thames; he may have caught pneumonia, or possibly it was appendicitis, acute indigestion, or most likely a stroke of apoplexy—at any rate, he was soon dead, much to the surprise of the nation. One of his last acts was to change his will to make his brother Gloucester 'Protector of the Realm,' in charge of his young nephews in the event of Edward's death; it's fair to say that Richard wouldn't be entirely diligent in that respect, nor exactly the best uncle who ever lived.

CHAPTER ELEVEN

The Winter of Our Discontent

In game theory, the term 'Hobbesian Trap' is applied to a situation in which two groups, out of a fear that the other will attack them, begin a spiral of preventive violence that becomes self-fulfilling. Named after miserable seventeenth-century philosopher Thomas Hobbes, its most famous example is World War I. It is also what happened in 1483, following Edward's death.

Thanks to Shakespeare, Richard III has gone down in history as one of the great villains of all time; besides perhaps King John, he is English history's greatest monster. As the play recalls, Edward IV was succeeded by his son, Edward V, who was just twelve, but on his way to London his party was met by his uncle Richard, who insisted on taking the boy into his care, had him declared illegitimate, and made himself king. Edward and his ten-year-old brother Richard were then placed in the Tower of London for their [Dr. Evil quotemarks] 'safekeeping' and never seen again, presumably murdered.

Shakespeare was writing under the patronage of Elizabeth I, whose grandfather Henry VII overthrew Richard, so the Tudors wished to portray the last Plantagenet as a monster. And Shakespeare was not alone; one chronicler, John Rous, wrote during

Henry VII's reign that 'Richard spent two whole years in his mother's womb and came out with a full set of teeth and hair streaming to his shoulders.' However, when Richard was alive, the same John Rous was writing glowing stuff about him, reporting that 'at Woodstock . . . Richard graciously eased the sore hearts of the inhabitants' by giving back common lands that had been taken by his brother and the king, offered money, and said he would rather have their hearts, reported Rous. Then, after Richard's death, Rous wrote of the old king: 'monster and tyrant, born under a hostile star and perishing like Antichrist.'

Shakespeare also implicates Richard in the killing of Somerset at St. Albans, when he was only two and a half. The playwright has him telling his father: 'Heart, be wrathful still: Priests pray for enemies, but princes kill.' So unless he was a real-life Stewie from *Family Guy*, we can assume this is not true.

Later, Richard, now aged seven, is seen persuading his father that it wouldn't be wrong to attack Henry VI. He says:

I cannot rest
Until the white rose that I wear be dyed
Even in the lukewarm blood of Henry's heart.

Which is quite precocious, if true.

The real Richard was a sickly child who was not expected to survive into his second decade; one chronicler remarked on the York children that 'Richard liveth yet.' He was the twelfth of thirteen children born to Richard of York and Cecily, and the fourth and youngest son to reach adulthood; he strongly resembled his father in looks and, although not tall and athletic like his brothers, some say he was attractive: Katherine, 'the old Countess of Desmond,' who apparently lived to the age of 140 early in James I's reign in the seventeenth century, claimed that as a girl she had danced with the Duke of Gloucester and 'he was the handsomest man in the room except his brother Edward, and was very well made.' Considering no one with modern health standards has lived anywhere near that age, she may possibly have been lying, just a bit.

And we now know that he did indeed have a curvature of the spine, which fitted in with Shakespeare's idea of him as a hunchback. Although five feet, eight inches, slightly above average height, the abnormality would have meant a reduction of a foot when standing, with his right shoulder higher than his left.[68] He also probably had a dry rasping cough because of roundworm, and a paranoid, uncomfortable manner; he fidgeted with his ring or the dagger on his belt, and chewed his lower lip when thinking. However, Thomas More said he could be merry and companionable.

Before 1483, Richard had been unwaveringly diligent and loyal to his brother, and as a result had become de facto ruler of the North. As a loyal administrator, he was so impressive that Edward named him lord protector in his will to look after the country until the new king was of age. Until his brother's death, he was popular, but this may have given him a fatal overconfidence, which, added to his burning hatred of the Woodville family, proved disastrous. Richard III had quite a few good points, although these tend to be overshadowed by the murdering-his-nephews business; he was a good soldier and administrator, very courageous, bright, and decisive, and his lawmaking was generally very sensible. He was highly religious, and had a particular devotion to St. Julian the Hospitaller, a first-century saint who killed his parents; he had a prayer to Julian in his Book of Hours that 'has a paranoiac quality,' in the words of one historian;[69] he was obsessed with the idea of disloyalty being all around him, and his motto was *Loyaute me lie* (loyalty binds me). Of Richard, being somewhat of the religious fanatic, More writes he posed 'as a goodly continent prince, clean and continent of himself, sent out of heaven into this vicious world for the amendment of men's mannes.'

Richard had spent some of his childhood in Yorkshire, and the Earl of Warwick was something of a father figure to him; he then married Warwick's daughter Anne, gaining much of Warwick's estate, and then, while aged nineteen, Richard had his widowed mother-in-law imprisoned in Middleham Castle, where she remained for the rest of her life. Richard and Anne had one son, born in 1476, called Edward, obviously. (Clarence also had a son called Edward and the stillborn boy whose death triggered his eventual insanity was called Richard.) The match said something of the incest of the time—as well as being brought up together, Richard was descended from Edward III through three different sons, his wife descended from him twice over.

The Coup

When Edward IV died, the Woodville clan didn't tell anyone for nine days, giving them time to put together their plans. The Woodvilles created a council, and Elizabeth's brother Edward raised a fleet that people feared could be used against domestic enemies. Rivers had been put in charge of Prince Edward's education, an obvious choice to help run the kingdom, being a scholar and sort-of mystic. References in declarations were made to the 'uterine brother' and 'uterine uncle,' while Richard of Gloucester was omitted. The coronation was set for May 4, after which the protector's authority ended; once that happened, the Woodvilles were in charge, which could be bad for their enemies, of whom the family had many; chief of them was Hastings.

Edward IV's will had demanded that Hastings make peace with the Marquess of Dorset, who was also married to Hastings's stepdaughter, but they 'maintained a deadly feud' over mistresses and land, being rivals in the midlands. Hastings had already lost his post as chamberlain and was worried that the Woodvilles would get rid of him if and when they took power; their mutual antagonism would be their mutual downfall. And so Hastings contacted Gloucester and urged him to come to London to prevent a Woodville coup, informing him of the whereabouts of Rivers.

Richard was now also approached by Henry Stafford, the Duke of Buckingham, who had a deep grudge against the Woodvilles and who turned out to be one of the least attractive characters of the entire conflict. Buckingham's father had been killed at St. Albans fighting for the king, and at the age of twelve he had become a ward of Elizabeth Woodville who married him to one of her numerous sisters, Catherine. Buckingham was therefore hugely resentful of the family.

Richard, Duke of Gloucester persuaded Rivers to wait for him so they could enter London together. They met on April 29 in Northamptonshire, where Gloucester, Buckingham, and Rivers had dinner in an inn, in a spirit of 'cheerful and joyous countenance.' However, the next day they were riding when Gloucester and Buckingham drew up and told Rivers and the queen's son Richard Grey they were under arrest; they were sent north and locked up in Warwick's old castle of Sheriff Hutton in Yorkshire.

When he caught up with the king, Richard explained to his nephew that he had arrested them to protect him; the boy did not believe him and although aged only twelve, knew what he was up to, but he could do nothing. And so Edward V entered London with Richard and Buckingham on May 4, the date he was supposed to have been crowned by the Woodvilles. Croyland wrote: 'With the consent and goodwill of all the lords, [Richard] was invested with power to order and forbid in every matter, just like another king. The king's name now appeared on charters: 'by the advise of oure derest oncle the duc of Gloucester, protectour and defensour of this our royalme during our yongage.'

Realizing the nightmare that was unfolding, Elizabeth Woodville fled to sanctuary in London with her younger son Richard, Duke of York, as well as her son by her first marriage, Thomas Grey, and a brother, Lionel Woodville. Another sibling, Edward Woodville, escaped to Brittany.

However, the lord protector, as Richard had been styled, intended to go further than Hastings had planned. Lord Stanley had a terrifying nightmare on June 12 that a savage boar slashed his and Hastings's heads with its tusks—a boar being Richard of Gloucester's badge. Badly shaken, he sent a message to his friend saying they should escape from the city. Hastings wasn't impressed, and replied: 'Tell him it is plain witchcraft to believe in such dreams.'

On Friday, June 13, Hastings, Archbishop of York Thomas Rotherham, and John Morton, bishop of Ely, were summoned for a council meeting at the Tower of London. Sir Thomas Howard, the Duke of Norfolk's son, went to Hastings's house to accompany him to the meeting, seemingly in a friendly, casual way; in fact, he had been sent by Richard to ensure Hastings went to his trap.

Richard joined the meeting at 9 a.m. then left and came back at 10:30 'with a sour and angry countenance' demanding to know what the penalty should be for anyone planning 'the destruction of me, being so near of blood to the king, and protector of this royal realm.' Hastings replied that this would, of course, be treason. Richard then showed everyone his arm, which was deformed and withered, and which he blamed on Elizabeth Woodville, and armed men came running into the room. Mancini wrote: 'Thereupon the soldiers, who had been stationed there by their lord, rushed in with the Duke of Buckingham, and cut down Hastings on the false pretext of treason; they arrested the others, whose life, it was presumed, was spared out of respect for religion and holy orders.' Richard shouted 'I arrest thee traitor' at Hastings, a soldier attacked Stanley and he, Morton, and Rotherham were taken off. Hastings was immediately beheaded. 'Thus fell Hastings, killed not by those enemies he had always feared, but by a friend whom he had never doubted,' Mancini reflected.

After the execution, Richard did not attain Hastings's widow or children, and none of them suffered financially, as was usually the case with traitors; he killed Hastings simply because he knew he would never back the next stage of his coup. Morton was imprisoned by Buckingham, while for some reason Stanley managed to escape punishment.

In another fateful move, on June 16 the archbishop of Canter-bury convinced the queen to hand over her younger son Richard for the coronation ceremony. The following day the coronation was canceled.

Richard had maneuvered to have the king proclaimed illegit-imate and instead claimed the throne for himself. A supportive theologian, Ralph Shaw, brother of the mayor of London, gave a sermon at St. Paul's on June 22 in which he declared that Edward's marriage to Woodville was illegal because he had been engaged to Lady Eleanor Butler, so making his children illegitimate. Rich-ard's sidekick Buckingham went even further by proclaiming that Edward IV was actually illegitimate because his mother had had an affair with an archer; Richard wasn't so keen on that one, and the allegation was quickly dropped. A legal document was drawn up, *Titulus Regius*, justifying Gloucester's claim to the throne on account of the Butler engagement; soon a group of leading men came to offer the crown to Richard who made a token objection before quickly accepting.

Richard's coronation was a grand affair in which king and queen walked barefoot to Westminster Abbey, where they stood naked from the waist up as they were anointed, with crowns placed on their heads. Richard, it was noticed by a witness, had a 'short and sour countenance'—a common theme—and looked around nervously during the ceremony. After forty-six courses were con-sumed at the banquet, the moralizing king had Edward's former mistress Jane Shore clapped in irons for her iniquity and forced to make a walk of atonement through London, although it backfired as the mostly male crowd felt sorry for her. Shore, as a Freewoman of London, was also able to choose her prison—she went for Ludgate Gaol as it had nice big windows and friends were allowed to bring food.

Buckingham claimed in a speech that the late king had paid more attention to 'Shore's wife, a vile and abominable strumpet, than to all the lords in England except unto those that made her their protector.' But everyone laughed at the authorities now being morally outraged by Edward's infidelities, and More wrote sardonically: 'And for this cause (as a goodly, continent prince, clean and faultless of himself, sent out of heaven into this vicious world for the amendment of men's manners), he caused the bishop of London to put her to open penance.' Richard, he wrote, 'taught others to exercise just and good which he would not do himself.'[70] As for Edward's womanizing, 'This fault not greatly grieved his people,' it was recorded.

Richard III had, in fact, fathered two or three children outside of marriage, most precious being John of Pontefract, whom he knighted in 1483 and acknowledged as 'our dear bastard son.' The poor bastard was beheaded in 1499.[71] Another, Katherine Plantagenet, married William Herbert, Earl of Huntingdon, one of Richard's supporters. But they were conceived when Richard was a young bachelor and it was assumed a young aristocratic man would get a few women pregnant.

Richard now had Rivers executed, as well as several other leading nobles. In his final days, Anthony Woodville, the renaissance man, wore a hair shirt and wrote a poem, 'a 'death day ballad,' which was 'Somewhat musing, And more mourning.' Mancini wrote of him: 'However much he prospered, he never harmed anyone, while doing good to many. Lord Rivers was always considered a kind, serious and just man, and tested by every vicissitude of life.'

The Princes in the Tower

Later in the summer, King Richard committed the most monstrous crime, for which he is still best known, although much of it remains a mystery. Following the coronation, Edward, twelve, and his ten-year-old brother Richard were placed in the Tower and seen less and less; from July, they were spotted only occasionally and, after September 28, when they were once witnessed playing in the

Tower, they were never seen again. At some point, they were moved to the inner Tower, and an Italian visitor noted that many thought they were dead and were too upset to talk about it. People clearly believed Richard to be responsible. In the fall, there was a plot to free the boys involving up to fifty London men; the conspirators were from humble backgrounds, and it seems to have been a spontaneous movement by ordinary Londoners in response to popular outrage at what Richard was doing. Four men were beheaded.

At an address to the Paris Estates General in January 1484, the chancellor of France mentioned that the English king had 'done away with his nephews,' and the French had denounced Richard taking the throne as 'orgies of crime.' This was certainly widely believed in England and Richard was hated as a result. The fact that he could not produce the boys when it was in his interest to do so suggests his guilt.

Yet despite this, various people still believe Richard to be innocent; in fact, of all historical figures, he has probably the largest personal following. The Richard III Society is bigger than that attached to any other individual monarch and has members as far away as Japan—even though he almost certainly did murder his young nephews. The Ricardian movement began in the early twentieth century, but its peak came after World War II with a biography by Paul Murray Kendall, and the 1951 detective novel, *The Daughter of Time*, in which a policeman manages to prove the king's innocence; in fact, in 1984, Richard was tried by a TV show, which found him not guilty, and if history has taught us anything, it's that trial by television works. Kendall suggested it was Buckingham, who had full access to the Tower, who was likely responsible and that he framed Richard. He also pointed to the fact that Henry VII made almost no effort to blame his predecessor for the princes' deaths even though he had every incentive to do so.

Ricardians are especially popular in the North of England, where Richard was well liked throughout his reign. He was the only king to have been raised in the region and to have spoken with a northern English accent; by 1484, two-thirds of sheriffs south of the Thames and Severn were Northerners, perhaps the only time in English history they have ruled over the South.

One of the only intimates of Richard to survive his downfall was his henchman James Tyrell; he was literally a 'henchman,' which was then a particular title for someone who looked after horses, rather than a thick-skulled hoodlum with a Brooklyn accent who says 'yeah boss.' Tyrell was executed for treason in 1502, and before his death he confessed to the killings, so booking himself a place as a Shakespearean villain. Whether he actually did it, we'll never know.

In 1674, workmen at the Tower dug up the skeletons of two children, and it was concluded they were those of the two princes; in July 1933, the urn was opened and dentists looked at their teeth, estimating that they were twelve to thirteen and ten, which would be consistent with their being murdered in 1483.

Buckingham rebellion

Dr. Morton had been placed in the custody of Buckingham, but in a strange twist, he now persuaded the Duke to rebel against the king. Buckingham was vain and foolish, and had dubious motives for turning against Richard; most likely he was stunned by how unpopular the new regime was and didn't want to go down with it. Buckingham, aided by Dorset, aimed to launch simultaneous uprisings in Wales, East Anglia, and the Southeast, and there were numerous people involved in the plot, as Richard was by now widely hated, among them a previously obscure Lancastrian nobleman, Henry Tudor, and Thomas Nandike, 'a 'necromancer of Cambridge.'

The king was furious when he found out, and in his proclamation from Lincoln on October 11 he called Buckingham 'the most untrue creature living whom with god's grace we shall not be long till we will be in that part and subdue his malice.' He denounced his enemies as 'traitors, sorcerers, lechers, misers, and evil councillors.' The proclamation against Dorset read that he 'hath many and sundry maids, widows, and wives damnably and without shame devoured, deflowered and defiled' while rebels were guilty of 'the damnable maintenance of vices and sin as they had in times past, as to great displeasure of God and evil example of all Christian people.'

However, if Richard was a hated tyrant, then Buckingham was not exactly a national darling either, and he failed to get support from his own tenants because he was a 'sore and hard-dealing man.' After Richard proclaimed a pardon for any of the common soldiers who laid down their arms, it's a sign of how unpopular Buckingham was that afterwards there were no Welsh names listed among those attained. The Duke of Buckingham's army disappeared, and one of his men betrayed him when he pretended to be a laborer.

In fairness, it was also ruined by the weather, especially the rain, in a typically British way. He went from Brecon to Herefordshire, but rainstorms flooded the road and river crossings, making progress impossible. Buckingham anyway failed to rouse the people of Herefordshire and so fled to Shropshire to his servant Ralph Bannister, an old friend since childhood. Bannister, however, almost immediately sold him out, and the Duke was captured and taken to Salisbury. There, he confessed 'without torture,' begging for his life and losing all dignity in his terror-stricken last few days; he was beheaded on November 2, and his skeleton was later found under a pub called the Saracen's Head many years later (in fact, it's one of three places to claim his burial site).

The rebels were hunted down although many escaped, among them one Cornish knight, Sir Richard Edgcumbe, who made a dramatic escape; he was chased through woods near his home of Cotehele in the Tamar gorge, with Richard's men close behind, 'fast at his heels,' when he found a big stone and put his cap on top, then rolled it over into the sea. With a big splash, his pursuers 'looking down after the noise and seeing his cap swimming, thereon supposed that he had desperately drowned himself, gave over their further hunting.'[72] Morton also managed to escape to the coast where he fled to the continent; Henry Tudor, having sailed from Brittany to Plymouth, spotted men on the coast who claimed to be Buckingham's troops, but being suspicious, sailed off; wisely, as it was a trap.

In January 1484, there were Attainders against Richard's growing list of enemies—Thomas Grey, Morton, Lionel Woodville, Peter Courtenay, bishop of Exeter, and Tudor's mother Margaret Beaufort. Beaufort escaped too much trouble from Richard III because, as Vergil says, 'the working of a woman's wit was thought of small account'; she was also married to Lord Stanley, who was too powerful to alienate. Her income and estates were therefore given to her husband and he was ordered to keep her isolated somewhere secret where her son could not contact her.

Most of those captured were beheaded, although Sir Ralph Ashton, nicknamed 'the Black Knight' for his armor and ruthlessness, supposedly condemned his victims to be rolled down hills in barrels with spikes inside. Worst still awaited Sir William Collingbourne, who was arrested for writing a ditty that went: 'The Catte, the Ratte and Lovell our dogge rulyth all Englande under a hogge.' Richard's banner was a boar and the people of London called him 'the Hog' behind his back, and his cronies Francis Lovell, William Catesby, and Richard Ratcliffe were nicknamed the Dog, the Cat, and the Rat. Collingbourne, unfortunately, was also discovered to have been passing messages on behalf of Henry Tudor and so, unlike the other Buckingham rebels, was hanged, drawn, and quartered. He was almost dead from hanging, when he was hauled to his feet and thrown onto a table where his body was 'straight cut down and ripped' and castrated. The *Great Chronicle of London* wrote that the 'torment . . . was so speedily done' that he could look down as his executioner put his hand into his chest and pulled out his heart, at which point Collingbourne said the rather appropriate last words: 'Jesus, Yet more trouble!'

However, with his enemies defeated, Richard enjoyed a brief moment of peaceful rule; he was a very moral man personally, apart from the various murders obviously, and devoted to both the Church and his wife; incredibly for this period, he didn't even cheat on her. Despite—or perhaps because of—his huge unpopularity, Richard III was a sensible lawmaker, even if this was forced on him by his lack of legitimacy. Under his rule, he allowed each justice of the peace to grant bail to any felony. He outlawed forced loans. He exempted books from import duties, and ruled that every writer, printer, and bookbinder could do business 'of whatever nation or country he may or shall be.' There were laws protecting innocent men from predatory neighbors using perverted legal forms. Indictments brought by unqualified juries were declared void. In 1484, Parliament passed acts preventing an accused person's goods being forfeit before they were convicted and banning the benevolences introduced by Edward IV.

However, he remained an unpopular tyrant and over 1484–5 Richard was issuing pardons freely in the desperate hope of winning over his enemies, among them John Morton, which was ignored. In total, five hundred men had fled to the continent after the Buckingham rebellion, where Henry Tudor now hosted a growing court of exiles around him, both Yorkists and Lancastrians. And so, in order to shore up his claim and unite this disparate group, on Christmas Day 1483 at Vannes Cathedral, Tudor swore to marry Edward's daughter Elizabeth of York and end the war between Lancaster and York.

Chapter Twelve

My Kingdom for a Horse

Henry Tudor's claim to the throne was very tenuous, but he had an advantage over most of the others in not being dead. Despite being from the illegitimate Beaufort line, he was enough of a threat that Edward IV offered a huge reward for his capture, although he was safe as long as the Duke of Brittany protected him; unfortunately, the Duke was, like many of the rulers at the time, periodically insane so he could not always be relied on.

Shakespeare presented Tudor as a heroic figure who came along to save the day, but in real life he was not especially popular or loved or even liked as king. A man with small, shrewd eyes 'and noticeably bad teeth in a long, sallow face beneath very fair hair,' Henry Tudor had lived rather against the odds and grew into an understandably cautious man. Still, he won, and that's what matters when it comes down to it.

After Henry V's death, his widow Catherine of Valois had become close to Edmund Beaufort, the future Duke of Somerset who was five years her junior. Edmund was also the nephew of Cardinal Henry Beaufort, then the archenemy of Humphrey of Gloucester, and so in 1427, under Gloucester's influence, Parliament spitefully forbade queens from remarrying without 'special licence' of an adult king for the sake of 'the preservation of the honor of the most noble estate of queens of England.' Since Catherine's son was six at the time, this made things rather difficult for her.

Catherine was described as being 'unable to fully curb her carnal passions,' but the position of a young dowager queen was a difficult and sometimes perilous one, doubly so if she were foreign. Her sexual habits were of prime interest to the Crown, as any lover or spouse would be raised to great power. Henry V's widow therefore shocked those around her by secretly marrying a man who was not only not of noble blood but also Welsh, viewed as barbarians at the time.

Owain Tudor was Catherine's footman, and according to one version she used to spy on the Welshman as he bathed naked in the Thames, or alternatively she noticed him when he fell asleep drunk on her lap—British men are so romantic, which women find irresistible. The Tudors had served the princes of Gwynedd and later the English kings. Owain's grandfather had been Tudur (Theodore) ap Goronwy, a nobleman from Anglesey, a Welsh-speaking region of the country, but his father Merdeddap Tudur, along with his brothers, had sided with Owain Glyndwr in his revolt, and while he had inherited his father's land, many of his relations had been excluded and they remained poor; Owain had risen through society solely by his soldiering ability and charm, serving in France for many years.

At some point around 1430, Catherine and Owain were married, although they were certainly an odd couple; she came from the royal family of Christendom's leading power, the heirs of Charlemagne, while he . . . did not. One evening, Owain brought his cousins John ap Maredudd and Hywel ap Llywelyn ap Hywel to meet the queen but they only spoke Welsh and Catherine said, 'they were the goodliest dumb creatures that she ever saw.'

After three or four children, Catherine died in 1437 and her sons Edmund and Jasper at the ages of seven and six went to work for Katherine de la Pole, abbess of Barking and the sister of the Duke of Suffolk. She was an influential figure who was godmother to the children of many wealthy families, and the abbey served as a sort of proto-boarding school. The Tudor boys spent five years at Barking, and as they got older, the king became closer to his half brothers. Blacman wrote that Henry VI put the Tudors under 'strict and safe guardianship' and 'before he was married, being as a youth a pupil of chastity . . . would keep careful watch through hidden windows of his chamber, lest any foolish impertinence of women coming into the house grow to a head, and cause the fall of any of his household.' The two teenage boys must have really thanked him for that.

In November 1452, the Tudor lads were raised to the peerage, Edmund as Earl of Richmond and Jasper Earl of Pembroke. They were also made legitimate half brothers of the king, while Parliament praised the 'famous memory' of their mother and 'all the fruit which her royal womb produced.' Jasper was given land seized by Yorkists, while Edmund managed to get himself engaged to the first Duke of Somerset's daughter Margaret Beaufort, the richest heiress in the kingdom.

Margaret's childhood had been grim even by the standards of the day; her father committed suicide before her first birthday, so she became a ward of the Earl of Suffolk, and he arranged her marriage to his son when he was just two and she one. Now, after Henry VI had dissolved that union, she was married off at twelve to Edmund Tudor and was pregnant at thirteen. This is even worse than it sounds, as girls matured later then (diet being poorer), and it was customary to wait until at least a girl's fourteenth birthday before consummating a marriage, for health reasons; she also had a slight frame, and as a result had a difficult pregnancy; she almost died in childbirth, as did her sickly baby, and was unable to conceive again. It's most likely Tudor did this out of greed rather than lust, for once she had given him a child, he owned her land forever, and maybe he didn't want to risk her dying in the meantime; either way, it doesn't present him in a great light. Not that Edmund got to enjoy the rewards, as he was already dead by this stage, having expired in captivity at the hands of his rival 'Black William' Herbert, who was from the most powerful Yorkist family in Wales.

Just two months after giving birth, Margaret rode to the home of the powerful Duke of Buckingham and negotiated a marriage with his second son, Henry Stafford, which was happy enough, although she rarely saw her own child. When Henry Tudor was only four, the Yorkists overthrew his uncle and the same William Herbert was able to buy his wardship for one thousand pounds, giving him tutors and grooming him for marriage. According to Polydore Virgil, he was 'kept as prisoner' by Herbert, although well looked after by his wife Anne Devereux; it was around this time he learned Welsh. The Herberts had also bought the wardship of the young Earl of Northumberland, whose father had just died at Towton. At the age of twelve, Henry was taken by Herbert to the Battle of Edgecote Moor to watch him take on Warwick, but unfortunately Herbert was on the losing side and afterward he was beheaded. Not the ideal awkward stepfather/stepson day out.

After Tewkesbury, Henry and his uncle Jasper fled to the continent and spent the next few years in exile in Brittany, under the protection of Duke Francis. They were kept in the capital Vannes, in a palace with a tennis court and fine stables, but in reality they were prisoners of Francis and depended on his goodwill, and, in 1476, the Duke agreed to send him back to Edward; Henry feigned an attack of fever, and fled to sanctuary in a church to recover— by the time he came out, Francis had changed his mind. It was a lucky escape. Meanwhile, Margaret Beaufort had been brought into the Yorkist circle. When, in 1476, Richard of York was reburied in Fotheringhay, Margaret attended to Queen Elizabeth; then after the birth of Edward and Elizabeth's daughter Bridget in 1480, Margaret carried the baby to the christening. Soon, there was talk of Henry Tudor marrying Edward IV's daughter Elizabeth, and it was only the king's premature death that ruined this.

After the Buckingham rebellion, Henry had another lucky escape when the Bretons—during one of Francis's bouts of insanity—again agreed to hand him over to the English. Morton had heard about the plans, most likely through Stanley, and was able to warn Tudor before he was taken. Instead, Henry and Jasper both snuck off the road, changed their clothes in some forests, and escaped into French territory; when Francis regained himself, he welcomed Henry back and apologized with a gift.

Richard, meanwhile, met with disaster in April 1484 when his only son died, leaving both parents devastated, and perhaps Richard feeling it was divine retribution. By the end of 1484, Anne Neville was dying, too, and Richard's behavior to his wife during her final weeks was of a new order of derangement; he spread a rumor that she had already died, knowing that the story would get back to her, so she would think he was trying to kill her. Richard hoped this would finish her off, for now that their son was dead he needed to be rid of her to make way for a new wife. He also refused to share her bed, although since she most likely had tuberculosis this was quite sensible.

To fight off the Tudor threat he considered taking a new wife, one bizarre option being Elizabeth of York. Sure she was his niece, and she looked just like her father, and he'd murdered both her brothers, but perhaps they could get over these stumbling blocks. Whether or not this was just black propaganda, Richard was forced to deny rumors he planned to marry Elizabeth, after Ratcliffe and Catesby warned the king that if this happened the North would rebel. He declared: 'It is so that divers seditious and evil disposed persons (both in our city of London and elsewhere within this our realm) enforce themselves daily to sow seed of noise and disclaundre against our person, and against many of the lords and estates of our land, to abuse the multitude of our subjects and avert their mind from us,' blaming it all on 'seditious persons.' (He liked long rambling letters, like his father.)

The king's paranoia had now reached fever pitch. After the rebellion, Vergil said, Richard became 'as yet more doubting than trusting in his own cause, was vexed, wrested and tormented in mind with fear.' Thomas More said of Richard that 'when he went abroad [outside], his eyes whirled about; his body privily fenced [secretly armed], his hand ever on his dagger, his countenance and manner like one already ready to strike again.' He 'rather slumbered than slept, troubled with fearful dreams.'

In June 1485, the king issued a proclamation against the threat of invasion, warning of 'the disinheriting and destruction of all the noble and worshipful blood of this Realm forever' if Tudor invaded. Vergil said he was 'vexed, wrested, and tormented in mind with fear.'

Bosworth

In August 1485, Tudor finally landed with a small force in Wales, his ancestral home, where he recited Psalm 43: 'Judge me, O Lord, and plead my cause.' He had recruited 'some three thousand of the most unruly men that could be found and enlisted in Normandy,'[73] his army filled with 'the worst sort,' men 'raised out of the refuse of the people,' among them two thousand Frenchmen and Bretons recently released from prison, as well as one thousand Scots and four hundred Englishmen. When they arrived in Britain, the Welsh and French troops had to be separated to stop them fighting, and local commander Sir Rhys Ap Thomas detested his allies so much he wished 'soundly to cudgel those French dogs.'

In the Powys town of Machynlleth, Tudor visited a bard, Dafydd Llwyd, who was also a noted clairvoyant. Asked whether Henry would be victorious, Dafydd was nervous about giving the wrong answer and so told him he'd give a reply the following day. Looking anxious in bed, Dafydd's wife asked him what was wrong and told him the answer was obvious: tell him he would succeed, because if he was right he'd be rewarded, and 'if not, you need not fear that he will return here to reproach you for being a false prophet.'[74]

Richard, hearing about the invasion, dictated a ranting letter on August 11 saying, 'And forasmuch as our rebels and traitors accompanied with our ancient enemies of France and other strange nations departed out of the water of Seine the first day of this present month.' He had stationed men across the West to intercept the force; however, after crossing the border, Henry's army was met by Thomas Mitton, who was in charge of Cawes on the Welsh marches and had pledged to Richard that an army would pass 'only over his belly.' Henry asked him to lie on his back so he could keep to his oath: 'upon this they entered and in passing through the said Mitton lay along the ground and his belly upward and so the said Earl stepped over him and saved his oath.'[75]

Meanwhile, the king's demand for military support was widely ignored. The Duke of Norfolk, one of the three largest magnates left, sent a letter to John Paston that concluded: 'Wherefore I pray you that you meet with me at Bury . . . and that you bring with you such company of tall men as you may goodly make at my cost and charge, besides that which you have promised the king; and, I pray you, ordain them jackets of my livery, and I shall content you at your meeting with me,' signing off, rather strangely to modern ears, 'Your lover, J. Norfolk.'

During the Buckingham rebellion, Norfolk had written to Paston asking him to bring 'six tall fellows in harness,' but he'd ignored him then—and did so once again. The Pastons had taken part in many of the battles in the war, including Towton and Barnet, but like most people they'd had enough. The same went for the House of Percy. The Earl of Northumberland turned up for the battle but just stood there doing nothing; after most of the Percy males had been killed fighting, it occurred to them it might be better to focus on things like landscape gardening.[76] Compared to earlier battles, Bosworth was very small; some, because of their position or connections, were forced to fight but there was little enthusiasm, and with all civil wars, it brought painful personal divisions: Sir Gervase Clifton and John

Byron were neighbors and friends in Nottinghamshire who fought
on different sides of the battle, Clifton for Richard and Byron for
Henry. They had an agreement that whoever survived would look
after the other's family (they both did, as it happened).

While King Richard was in Nottingham, he was told that
Tudor had entered Shrewsbury and crossed the Severn. 'Suffering no inconvenience, he began to burn with chagrin,' a chronicler
reported, and promised to kill any knight or squire 'from the town
of Lancaster to Shrewsbury, leaving none alive' and promising to lay
waste 'from the holy-head to St. David's Land, where now be tow-
ers and castles high' reducing them to 'parks and plain fields.' This
reference to Lancashire was probably because he suspected Thomas
Stanley of treason. In fact, Stanley, who always got away with playing both sides, was now in a very difficult position; his son Lord
Strange was arrested and confessed that he and his uncle William
were working for Tudor, but Lord Strange insisted that his father
was loyal; Stanley expressed surprise his son was imprisoned as he
had never dealt 'with traitory,' although he was obviously lying.

The two armies were camped near Bosworth, just outside
Leicester, on the site of a plague village, one of three thousand that
had disappeared in the fourteenth century. There had been numerous defections in the previous days, with soldiers sneaking out of
Richard's camp to escape battle or to join Tudor. A poem was stuck
on Norfolk's tent the night before, warning that there would be a
deal to uncrown the king:

> Jockey of Norfolk, be not too bold
> For Dickon thy master is bought and sold.

The day before battle, Richard's crown was also stolen by a
Scots Highlander called MacGregor, when he explained that—
as his mother had prophesized—he would be hanged, he thought
it may as well be for something memorable, the king was amused

enough to pardon him. What his eventual fate was is unknown—probably hanging for something really humdrum and banal.

The king was eager for battle with Tudor, despite the odds beginning to turn against him, and may well have wished for his reckoning, one way or the other. Historians tend to make a great deal of the fact that Richard was plagued by bad dreams the night before battle, sometimes taken as proof of a bad conscience, though with four thousand soldiers marching his way, it's hardly surprising.

In the morning, Richard addressed his Spanish servant: 'Salazar, God forbid I yield one step. This day I will die as king or win.' Richard then gave a speech before battle attacking the 'unknown Welshman, whose father I never knew, nor him personally saw,' who intended to 'overcome and oppress' the country with 'a number of beggarly Bretons and fainthearted Frenchmen.'

Lord Stanley, meanwhile, had claimed to not be able to come because he had the highly contagious and fatal sweating sickness. The king threatened to execute his son, whom he now held as hostage, to which the lord replied: 'Sire, I have other sons.' Stanley said he'd join the king 'at some suitable junction' (i.e., when he was winning), but in the end Richard's aides persuaded him not to execute Lord Strange, or they didn't carry it out because they figured that Tudor might win. And so Stanley got away with it again.

Realizing that the Lancashire lord would betray him, Richard ordered Northumberland to place his troops between the Stanleys and Tudors. He then led his knights into the battle 'all inflamed with ire' and decided he would lead from the front, wearing his helmet with a royal, golden crown on top, even though his advisers had warned him it would mark him out. In a furious charge downhill, the king killed Henry's banner-bearer with his lance, and knocked another man out of the saddle with a battle-ax. He may even have fought with Tudor who was almost killed; at one point Henry's men 'were now almost out of hope of victory.'

Stanley's affinity was uncommitted until it was clear which side was winning, and only then did he join his stepson. Then at some point, King Richard was brought down and the back of his head was chopped off, most likely by a Welsh soldier. His last words weren't 'my kingdom for a horse,' but 'Treason! Treason!'—although Richard's horse, White Surrey, was also cut down. Vergil wrote: 'King Richard, alone, was killed fighting manfully in the thickest press of his enemies.' He preferred to die rather than flee, he recorded, and shouted: 'I will die king of England, I will not budge a foot.' He was, in fact, the last king of England to die in battle, a record he probably won't lose for some time.

Afterwards, his body was stripped naked, 'nought being left about him so much as would cover a privy member,' and the body was horribly mutilated. The chronicler of Crowland remarked dryly of the abuse of Richard's corpse: 'many other insults were heaped upon it . . . not exactly in accordance with the laws of humanity.' Someone found the crown in the field, and Stanley, the luckiest man around, happened to be at the right place at the right time to crown Tudor as King Henry VII. Northumberland, having watched the thing without helping, slunk off home with his men.

Not everyone was happy about the result. The Recorder of York wrote in the city records: 'This day was it known that King Richard, late mercifully ruling over us was piteously slain and murdered, to the great hevines of this citie.' It wasn't until October 22 that authorities in the town, the north's largest, formally acknowledged Henry as king by dating their minutes by his reign.

Richard had spent his last night at the nearby White Boar, and after the battle the innkeeper hastily repainted it and renamed it the Blue Boar, which just happened to be the badge of the Earl of Oxford—the site is now a Travelodge, a chain of hotels.[77] Henry marched south toward the capital with his French and Breton troops, where they were met by the city's leading dignitaries—most of whom would be dead within weeks.

The Tudors

That year most people would have been less concerned about who was the king than with a ghastly new disease, the Sweating Sickness or 'English Sweats,' most likely brought by Henry's soldiers. The Sweats killed two mayors of London and six aldermen in just one week; Mayor William Stokker lasted only four days in the role. The infected burned with uncontrollable temperatures and thirst so bad they ripped the clothes from their bodies even in the freezing cold. Then they died, usually.

Tudor's triumph meant the end of the War of the Roses, although no one knew it at the time, or referred to it as such, or had a concept of the 'Tudor era.' Long into the reign of his monstrous son Henry VIII there was still the fear of further dynastic threats, which is why the two Henrys, father and son, killed so many of their relatives. As one of his first acts, Henry VII had twenty-eight people attained on high treason after passing a law stating that his reign had begun on the eve of Bosworth, which therefore made anyone who fought for Richard a traitor. There was widespread outrage at this trick; however, the new king showed clemency to the defeated, the exception being the hated Catesby who was executed. He left a moving letter to his wife with a passive-aggressive request to the Stanleys that they 'help and pray for my soul for ye have not for my body as I trusted in you.'

After the necessary papal dispensation was received, Henry VII married Elizabeth of York in February 1486, and later that year a son, Arthur, was born, his name a tribute to the king's Welsh ancestry. Henry and Elizabeth's descendants still rule the country today.

The new regime meant great rewards for the supporters of Tudor. His uncle Jasper, who had spent most of his life in poverty, now became one of the richest men in England. He was made Duke of Bedford, Earl of Pembroke, and lieutenant of Calais, lord-lieutenant of Ireland, and earl marshal of England and went by the title 'The high and mighty Prince Jasper, brother and uncle of kings.'

The loyal Lancastrian Earl of Oxford got back all his estates, but he was magnanimous to his enemies, including the son of his archenemy the Duke of Norfolk. Norfolk's daughter-in-law Lady Surrey wrote that 'I have found mine lord of Oxenford singular very good and kind lord to mine and lord and me . . . For him I dreaded most and yet, as hithero, I find him best.' Oxford also took in a former comrade, Lord Beaumont, after he went mad.

Poor Jane Shore ended up a beggar, 'nothing left but ravelled skin and hard bone,' the men in her life all violently dead and her 'unfriended and worn out of acquaintance.' The Earl of Northumberland, despite his attempts to avoid conflict, was eventually beaten to death by a mob in North Yorkshire, still angry that he had deserted Richard III.

Margaret Beaufort, who had endured an incredibly tough life, now found herself a very powerful and rich queen mother. One of her first jobs was to take care of Clarence's son, the hapless Edward, Earl of Warwick, who had the best claim to the throne but most likely had some sort of intellectual deficiency (the constant inbreeding probably didn't help). Despite his feeble state, Warwick was always a problem, and when rumors broke out that Tudor had been defeated at Bosworth, there were protests in favor of him.

Beaufort retired to Collyweston in Northamptonshire where she became a sort of nun and took a vow of chastity, keeping an entire choir, with a dozen boys and four men at her own personal chapel. She confessed twice each week and ended up damaging her back from kneeling so much in church. Her confessor was one Dr. John Fisher, a future cardinal, 'an awesomely austere figure' who had a skull placed on the altar whenever he said Mass and on dining tables during food. He ended up being executed by her grandson Henry VIII in 1535.

Margaret Beaufort herself died after eating a cygnet, a baby swan, which is ironic as it was her son who made all swans the property of the crown, which is still a well-known and eccentric law today in England.[78] In recognition of his mother's ancestry, Henry VII adopted the Beaufort family symbol of the Portcullis—a medieval gate—as his own, which is how it came to be used to symbolize the House of Commons.

Although Bosworth looks like the finale in hindsight, the dynastic conflict dragged on for a while. Richard's heir had been his sister's son John de la Pole, Earl of Lincoln, and he remained a threat, so that Tudor, after Bosworth, spread a rumor he had been killed to stop any immediate uprising in his favor. There was actually yet another battle in 1487, the little known Swiss invasion of Britain which culminated at the Battle of Stoke Field; although forgotten about, Stoke was probably bigger than Bosworth.

It began with a pretender to the throne called Lambert Simnel who turned up in Dublin claiming to be Clarence's son Warwick, even though the real Warwick was, if not well, then alive. Simnel was from a humble background, the son of an organ builder, but at the age of ten he was taken in by a priest called Richard Simons. The slightly dubious cleric noticed Simnel had a strong resemblance to the princes in the tower and so groomed him to talk like an aristocrat in order to pretend to be Richard. However, at some point Simons heard that Warwick had died in custody and so changed the story.

Despite this rather implausible tale and, as it turns out, Warwick still being alive, Simnel was accepted by a number of aristocrats. He turned up in Dublin, where the leading nobleman in Ireland, the Earl of Kildare, got behind him and at Christ Church Cathedral he became the only English 'king' crowned in Ireland as Edward VI. He was also supported by John de la Pole, who planned to simultaneously invade and also claimed to have helped this 'Warwick' escape from the Tower. Presumably, he hoped to become king himself.

Henry, always paranoid, could never trust anyone, although quite sensibly; when the invasion came he had the Marquess of

Dorset placed in custody and, when he complained, the king explained that if he were a true friend he wouldn't mind this precautionary measure. The king also distrusted Dorset's mother, his own mother-in-law Elizabeth Woodville, and now confiscated her widow's income and sent her to live with nuns in Bermondsey for the rest of her life.

At Stoke Field in Nottinghamshire, the mixed Swiss, German, and Irish army was defeated by Henry's troops; some four thousand invaders died in the battle, as did the Earl of Lincoln. Simnel was pardoned, and he ended up working as a cook in the royal household, living another thirty-five years. There was later a plot in favor of Warwick hatched by the monks of Abingdon in 1489; townsmen hanged an abbot, but a conspiring cleric, Abbot Sant, escaped and was pardoned four years later, on condition that he say a Mass daily for the king, a sort of joke on Henry's part. Then, in 1495, yet another pretender turned up with an army, this one even more improbable, a Belgian called Perkin Warbeck or Pierrequin Werbecque. The son of a boatman, Perkin had arrived in Ireland in 1491 and while walking through Cork was dressed in his master's clothes when someone pointed out that he resembled one of the princes in the tower (one theory about all these young men looking like the princes is that they might have been Edward's illegitimate sons). He was taught English and told to pretend to be Richard of York.

Warbeck invaded twice and was put in the Tower, but after trying to escape in 1499, he and the hapless Warwick were both executed. Poor Clarence's son was killed because Ferdinand of Aragon told Henry his son could not marry his daughter Catherine because the dynasty was insecure while there were Plantagenets still around. Afterward, Henry Tudor's son did get to marry Catherine of Aragon, and they lived happily ever after. Sort of.

The Stanley family luck also ran out. Sir William Stanley, who had helped put Tudor on the throne, wasn't given titles after 1485, partly because the king felt that he had been slow in helping him;

then his stance during the 1495 rebellion was ambiguous enough to get him executed.

Nineteenth-century constitutional expert Lord Mersey estimated that between 1400 and 1485 some four kings, twelve princes of the blood, and twelve close relatives were killed in battle, murder, or execution. The only Plantagenets in the male line to have survived the era are the Beauforts, descendants of John of Gaunt.[79] Among the later achievements of the family, the eighth duke of Beaufort popularized the Indian sport 'battledore and shuttlecock,' which became known after his stately home, Badminton House in Gloucestershire.

There were still plenty of people with royal blood left to kill, however. Lincoln's brother Edmund was executed in 1515. Another, Richard de la Pole, was killed at the Battle of Pavia in 1525. Henry, Marquess of Exeter, son of Edward IV's daughter Catherine, was sent to the block in 1538. Henry, Lord Stafford, was put to death in 1521. Clarence's daughter Margaret, Countess of Salisbury, was executed in 1541 by Henry VIII, three years after her son Henry de la Pole. The sixty-eight-year-old ran away and screamed around Tower Green until the guards pulled her down and took her head off. Margaret was executed because she had refused to accept her cousin breaking with the pope, the Reformation now giving the royal family a different reason to kill each other.

By then, Henry VIII had dissolved the monasteries, and the medieval period had truly given way to the early modern. Countless old religious institutions were left ruined, among them Greyfriars in Leicester, which was destroyed and the graves lost—among them that of Richard III. And yet, rather miraculously, the king's remains were discovered in 2012, under a car park, identified via the mitochondrial DNA of a male descendant from a direct female line of the king's sister, Anne, Duchess of Exeter. The king was finally buried in 2015 in a solemn ceremony in Leicester cathedral, and the following year Leicester City won the Premier League title, having had odds of over 5000/1, the biggest upset in English and possibly European soccer history. Some people attributed it to Richard III as a joke, the mayor of Leicester saying the city was being repaid for burying him.[80] (In fact he'd wanted to be buried at York.)

The end of the medieval era came with the fall of Constantinople in 1453, which led to an influx of Greek scholars into western Europe. Thirty years earlier, the Portuguese King Henry the Navigator, descended from Gaunt, had explored West Africa, the start of that country's incredible adventurers around the world, which further accelerated after the Ottoman Turks had cut off the East. In 1486, the Portuguese rounded Cape Horn, and just seven years after Bosworth this new age was ushered in when an explorer working for Spain set foot in the Americas. The modern world had begun. And so, for English history, Bosworth marks a convenient end to the medieval period, for although life went on for most people as before, the time of warring aristocrats was over. The future now belonged not to knights or barons or vengeful dukes, but to lawyers. Which was a good thing . . . sort of.

BIBLIOGRAPHY

This book is a short and simplified account of the period, which is well covered by historians in books and publications—at both academic and popular level—a very, very small sample of which can be found below.

Ackroyd, Peter. *Foundations.*

Ashley, Mike. *British Kings and Queens.*

Bryson, Bill. *Mother Tongue.*

Castor, Helen. *Blood and Roses.*

Castor, Helen. *Joan of Arc.*

Castor, Helen. *She-Wolves.*

Clarke, Stephen. *1000 Years of Annoying the French.*

Crystal, David. *The Stories of English.*

Duffy, Maureen. *England.*

Fraser, Antonia. *Kings and Queens of England.*

Gillingham, John. *Conquest, Catastrophe and Recovery.*

Gillingham, John. *The War of the Roses.*

Goodwin, George. *Fatal Colours.*

Harvey, John. *The Plantagenets.*

Hibbert, Christopher. *The English: A Social History.*

Holmes, George. *The Later Middle Ages 1272–1485.*

Jenkins, Simon. *A Short History of England.*

Jones, Dan. *The Hollow Crown.*

Jones, Terry. *Medieval Lives.*

Kendall, Paul Murray. *Richard the Third.*

Lacey, Robert. *Great Tales from English History.*

Manchester, William. *A World Lit Only by Fire.*

Mortimer, Ian. *The Time Traveller's Guide to the Middle Ages.*

Myers, A. R. *England in the Late Middle Ages.*

Neillands, Robin. *The Hundred Years War.*

Ormrod, W. H. *The Kings and Queens of England.*

Palmer, Alan. *Kings and Queens of England.*

Royle, Trevor. *The War of the Roses.*

Saul, Nigel. *For Honour and Fame.*

Schama, Simon. *A History of Britain.*

Seward, Desmond. *A Brief History of the Hundred Years War.*

Seward, Desmond. *A Brief History of the War of the Roses.*

Seward, Desmond. *Richard III.*

Seward, Desmond. *The Demon's Brood.*

Skidmore, Chris. *Bosworth: The Birth of the Tudors.*

Speck, W. A. *A Concise History of Britain.*

Strong, Roy. *The Story of Britain.*

Tombs, Robert. *The English and Their History.*

Tuchman, Barbara. *A Distant Mirror.*

Weir, Alison. *Lancaster and York.*

Whittock, Martyn. *A Brief History of the Life in the Middle Ages.*

Wilson, Derek. *Plantagenets.*

Endnotes

1. The White Hart remains the most popular today, being the symbol of Richard II, who passed the law forcing pubs to adopt names.
2. Another Scotsman, the philosopher David Hume, used the term 'The War Between the Two Roses' in his 1762 History of England. Nineteenth century writer Lady Maria Callcott is also attributed with the phrase the War of the Roses.
3. Dan Jones, *The Hollow Crown*.
4. If you ever visit England, you'll probably see this Tudor Rose at some point, it being the symbol of the English tourism board.
5. John Gillingham, *The War of the Roses*.
6. Desmond Seward, *A Brief History of the War of the Roses*.
7. Gillingham, *War*.
8. *Richard II*, Act II, Scene I.
9. The fact that the club, until 2017, played at White Hart Lane is just coincidence.
10. Strictly speaking, these were just wartime ordinances rather than actual Parliamentary laws. However, just to be sure, in 2012, Mr. Henry Shrimp wrote to York council asking whether it was still okay to kill Scotsmen after dark. They replied: 'After an extensive search of our records I can confirm that there are no records of any Scotsmen being legally shot with a bow and arrow in the last ten years. There is however a vague recollection of an alleged occurrence several centuries ago which involved a group of men from the Nottingham area, dressed in green, who were enjoying a stag night in York.' http://www.bbc.co.uk/news/uk-england-35376020.

11. In medieval England, all cities had curfews, being absurdly danger-ous, the bell of St. Mary-le-bow in Cheapside signaling London's; therefore, anyone who was born within earshot was said to be a true 'Cockney,' a word that derived in the medieval period for Londoners. Highgate is rather outside earshot, although pantos don't tend to be strictly accurate.

12. Martyn Whittock, *A Brief History of the Life in the Middle Ages*.

13. Terry Jones, *Medieval Lives*.

14. http://www.historyextra.com/article/military-history/10-facts-henry-v-and-battle-agincourt.

15. http://www.historyextra.com/feature/henry-v-cruel-king.

16. Seward, *War of the Roses*.

17. Robert Tombs, *The English and Their History*.

18. Any such reports involving high-powered women must be taken with a bit of salt, but the accounts of the Queen's debauchery are quite common.

19. Barbara Tuchman, *A Distant Mirror*.

20. Edouard Perroy, the twentieth-century French historian.

21. http://www.historyextra.com/feature/henry-v-cruel-king.

22. Tombs, *English*.

23. Desmond Seward, *A Brief History of the Hundred Years War*.

24. Gillingham, *War*.

25. Seward, *Hundred Years War*.

26. Tuchman, *A Distant Mirror*. This, however, is disputed; she certainly disinherited him, although whether that is the same thing is another question.

27. Helen Castor, *Joan of Arc*.

28. It became known as the French disease in Italy and Germany, although the French called it the Italian disease, the Dutch called it the Spanish disease, the Russians the Polish disease, and the Turks the Christian disease.

29. Castor, *Arc*.

30. The Earl of Salisbury, before half his head was blown off.

31. Castor, *Arc*.

32. Stephen Clarke, *1000 Years of Annoying the French*.

33. Edouard Perroy, the famous French medieval historian.

34. Castor, *Arc*.

35. Tombs, *English*.

36. Christopher Hibbert, *The English: A Social History*.

37. Hibbert, *The English*.

38. Paul Murray Kendall. 'And in the growing desire for privacy which the lords and his family found in privy chambers and solars, retreating from the hurly burly of communal life in the great hall.'

39. Robin Neillands, *The Hundred Years War*.

40. John Blacman wrote of him that 'he also customarily wore a long gown with a rolled hood like a townsman, and a full coat reaching below his knees, with shoes, boots and foot-gear wholly black, rejecting expressly all curious fashion of clothing.'

41. Gillingham, *War*.

42. Seward, *War of the Roses*.

43. Paul Murray Kendall, *Richard the Third*.

44. Seward, *Hundred Years War*.

45. https://nevillfeast.wordpress.com/2010/05/19/.

46. Lady Day was the origin of Mothering Sunday, or as it's called in the United States, Mother's Day, although Americans celebrate it in May. The English version falls nine months before Christmas Day.

47. In the 1990s, Julie Kirkbride, herself an MP, was married to Andrew Mackay MP, having been previously engaged to another Conservative MP, Stephen Milligan, who died in 1994 from autoerotic asphyxiation. Google it, I'd rather not explain.

48. This account was recorded in Robert O'Flanagan's 1870 biography of Edmund, and may be suspect. Numerous accounts in history, including Shakespeare's *Henry VI* and *Our Island Story*, portray Rutland as a mere boy, but at seventeen he would have already been a soldier and legitimate target in war.

49. Some historians suggest that there weren't actually any Scottish soldiers and this was all propaganda.

50. Seward, *Hundred Years War*.

51. He was the ancestor of the British Liberal party leader Jeremy Thorpe, who resigned in the 1970s following a typically British scandal that involved repressed homosexual love and dogs.

52. 'One battle took place in the snow; one in a thick early morning mist; another in a rain-storm.' Gillingham, *The War of the Roses*.

53. An English blizzard, that is, which by the standards of North Dakota would barely register.

54. George Goodwin, *Fatal Colours*.

55. D. R. Cook, *Lancastrians and Yorkists*.

56. Kendall, *Richard*.
57. http://www.british-history.ac.uk/camden-record-soc/vol17/pp210-239.
58. Simon Jenkins, *A Short History of England*.
59. This is admittedly a colorful version of events. What really took place, to paraphrase comedian Stewart Lee, was probably not quite as romantic.
60. Henry I's wife had been half-English but born in Scotland, and Henry IV's first wife had been English, but she died before he took the crown.
61. Seward, *War of the Roses*.
62. Alison Weir, *Lancaster and York*.
63. A contemporary, quoted in Paul Murray Kendall.
64. There is a minor character in Shakespeare's *Henry VI* based on a mixture of Tiptoft and another historical figure.
65. John Warkworth, writing in the fifteenth century.
66. Admittedly, it was Thomas More who first wrote this, and he was not exactly an impartial observer of Richard III; however, Gloucester was in charge of the Tower at the time, so it's not implausible.
67. Caxton's first edition of Chaucer recently sold for £4.6m in 1998, although as recently as May 2017, two pages of an 'incredibly rare' early Caxton manuscript were found in a library at Reading, and valued at £100,000. http://www.bbc.co.uk/news/education-39846929.
68. Chris Skidmore, *Bosworth: The Birth of the Tudors*.
69. Desmond Seward, *The Demon's Brood*.
70. From *The Great Chronicle of London*.
71. Possibly. The records are unclear.
72. According to their family tradition.
73. Skidmore, *Bosworth*.
74. Skidmore, *Bosworth*.
75. From *Bosworth*. As the author Chris Skidmore states, this story may be a bit colorful to be true.
76. In fact, the Percy family still raised their own army as late as the Napoleonic War, although their home is famous for its landscaped garden; in the eighteenth century, the grounds of Alnwick were sculpted by Capability Brown.
77. The pub was demolished in 1836, although a 'Richard III theme pub' of the same name is planned for Leicester city center.

78. Some hapless eastern European immigrants found themselves in trouble a few years back for killing what they presumed was a wild bird without being aware of this quaint English law. They became public enemies and were all over the tabloids.
79. Although recent DNA analyses suggests that they aren't in fact, and that along the way one of their number was cuckolded.
80. https://www.thesun.co.uk/archives/news/1156904/the-kings-power-did-the-digging-up-of-richard-iii-lead-leicester-to-the-premier-league-title/.